A CUP OF COMFORT®

for

Women

Stories that celebrate
the strength and grace
of womanhood

Edited by Colleen Sell

Aadamsmedia
Avon, Massachusetts

For Aunt Junella,
who showed me that laughter
does heal tears and light does extinguish darkness.

Published by
Adams Media, an F+W Publications Company
57 Littlefield Street, Avon, MA 02322. U.S.A.
www.adamsmedia.com and *www.cupofcomfort.com*
ISBN 10: 1-59869-662-9
ISBN 13: 978-1-59869-662-2

Printed in the United States of America.

J I H G F E D C B A

Library of Congress Cataloging-in-Publication Data
A cup of comfort for women: stories that celebrate the strength
and grace of womanhood / edited by Colleen Sell.
p.   cm.
1. Women—Religious life. I. Sell, Colleen.
BV4527 .C84 2002   158.1'28'0'82--dc21
2002008854

This book is available at quantity discounts for bulk purchases.
For information, please call 1-800-289-0963.

Acknowledgments

When I am in the throes of writing or compiling a book, I become completely engulfed in the process, oblivious to the enormity of the task. But at the very beginning of a book's development, when it is little more than a concept, and again upon its completion, I stand in awe of what will come and what has been done. It is then that I truly recognize and appreciate the collaborative endeavor that each book entails. And so, I extend my gratitude to every person who has contributed to the creation of this anthology—including those whose stories were not included. It takes courage to write and even more courage to put your stories on display for an editor and the world to judge. Bravo to you storytellers all!

To those courageous and talented souls whose stories we have had the privilege of publishing in this book: thank you, thank you, thank you!

To the hardworking, kindhearted, and accomplished staff at Adams Media Corporation: thank you for your extraordinary partnership. I am particularly indebted to Kate Epstein, Laura MacLaughlin, Kate McBride, Sophie Cathro, Gene Molter, Gary Krebs, and Bob Adams.

I am so grateful to my family and friends for their continued belief in me and for understanding when my work has taken my time and attention away from them. You are the treasures and the center of my life.

Most important, thank you, dear Readers, for allowing us to share this cup of comfort with you. May these stories bring you comfort and joy.

Contents

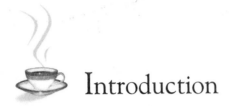 Introduction

Joy is the holy fire that keeps our purpose warm and our intelligence aglow.

~Helen Keller

Like most women of my generation and, I suspect, of generations before and since, I grew up in a culture that forwarded two defining notions about the female gender: Women are nurturers, and women are hard to please. The implication of these proclaimed truisms is that women are, by nature, a self-sacrificing and persnickety lot. I've never liked that image, and have refused to buy into it.

Though women do, indeed, have a long history of and an enormous capacity for taking care of others, there are remarkably few "miserable martyrs" among us. Women find joy and bring joy and create joy in their lives in myriad ways—including, but certainly not limited to, the joy that comes from giving, not only *of* oneself, but also *to* oneself.

That is not to say it is easy to nurture yourself while nurturing others. Many of our responsibilities *are* important, and some, like caring for our children, *do* take precedence. And you can only stretch a good woman so far. My sister has a magnet on her refrigerator, a gift from another single working mother, that reads: "I am woman . . . I am invincible . . . I am tired." That funny (as in ha-ha) isn't so fun when it's the reality of your life. For women accustomed to being last on their long list of priorities, taking care of themselves comes only after they've taken care of everything else—and for some, "after" rarely or never comes. The folly of self-neglect, of depriving oneself of peace and pleasure, is that it breaks us down and wears us out—and then we're unable to take care of anything or anybody.

It is essential to every woman's mental, physical, emotional, and spiritual well-being to infuse her life with frequent doses of the things that calm, restore, enrich, and delight her. Every woman is entitled to a life of abundance. Every woman is capable of being pleased and of pleasing herself. Creature comforts and life's riches abound. We have only to open the door and let them in.

Let your journey of self-nurturing begin here, or continue anew, with this collection of carefully selected stories about the many different people and experiences and things that bring comfort and joy to women. May this book bring you enjoyment and inspire you to let a little more sunshine into your life.

—*Colleen Sell*

On Turning Forty

I am turning forty, soon. And, as with other milestones in life, I feel the need to write about it. How do I feel? Well, I don't feel forty, that's the first thing. I feel good. Great, in fact. So, the number doesn't bother me. What does, is the decade that will surely follow. With every other decade I've had a distinct set of goals, things I felt I needed to accomplish in order to move on to the next phase of my life. Not so with my forties. So that leaves me feeling . . . uncertain. I've never not had something to go after. And that makes me something I'm not entirely familiar with: comfortable.

The twenties were, indeed, roaring for me. I didn't so much as bat an eye when I left nineteen behind (no doubt in a smoky bar on my college campus). I felt as if I had ten more years to party. As it turned out, I did. After college, the smoky bar turned into a beach as I took the growing-up show on the road and ended up in Southern California. What a ball I had discovering the beginning of adulthood. I worked at launching my career in advertising and worked harder still at packing the most fun I could into life. Birthdays came and went, and I could not have cared less.

When I looked in the mirror and saw a thirty-year-old, things got a little stickier. Then, I realized that time was of the essence if I was going to have everything I ever wanted: marriage, children, someone to make goofy cookies with. Southern California was everything I needed it to be as a young woman, but if I was going to accomplish my lifelong dreams, I'd better head back to the heartland. In the Midwest, chances were better that men not only would commit to a lunch date the following week, but might go for much more.

I was right. My thirties were very prolific. I met, lived with, married, and procreated—twice, in fact—with my wonderful husband. Now, I have my six-year-old marriage, four-year-old son, and two-year-old daughter to help me blow out forty candles. Whew.

Now what? If I were able to make a wish and to not be the introspective freak that I am, I'd wish to remain on this path I've made for myself. I'd like my marriage to remain intact, to maybe even breathe some life back into it now that I'm not a walking wet nurse. I'd like my children to continue to grow and amaze me with their fresh-faced enthusiasm. I'd like to continue juggling my friendships as best I can, considering that we all have young children who throw up on our black shirts just as we're trying to get out the door to meet each other. I'd really like to have the privilege of watching my mother grow older gracefully for many more years to come. These are goals, I suppose. But "maintenance" isn't something I can wrap my spirited, ambitious self around for the next ten years.

By this point in life, I know myself pretty well. I've come to accept that if I wasn't a size six at twenty, I can't expect to be a size six now. I know that if too many people are near me when I try to put on makeup, I start to sweat. I know what I can let go of and what I need to work out so that I don't feel anxious. And, I'm telling you, I need something that I can strive for during the next decade.

I'm a walker, a Forrest Gump–like walker who just doesn't know when to stop. One day, though, I did. Even though I hike the same trail through the same woods every single day, I saw a tree not unlike all the others, but on that day, it stood out to me. And so I stopped. Maybe it was the recent rain, maybe it was the fact that the yellow leaves had all but abandoned their job of announcing my birthday (autumn, to the rest of the world) and fallen at my feet. I don't know why, but in that instant, I knew what I was supposed to do with this next chapter of my life.

That tree stood out to me, because, overnight, the leaves had fallen and revealed what keeps it all together: its trunk, its backbone—lustrous and strong and reaching toward the sky. As I looked around, with both feet firmly planted on the ground, my woods were no longer a beautiful blur. They were vast and rich with possibilities. I felt a sense of discovery I hadn't had, or taken the time to have, in a very long time. It made me excited to go on. Even though I'd be moving in the same direction I'd been going all along, it would be with a new focus.

In my forties, I'm going to pay attention to something I'd almost lost track of: myself. I'll be moving forward, not only as someone's wife or mother, sister or daughter, writer or friend, but as the woman I've become somewhere along the way. In this decade, I intend to slow down and think and appreciate and learn. And even if I have no great new accomplishment to show for the next ten years, I know the process will be exhilarating.

—*Julie Clark Robinson*

A Bike with Pink Ribbons

The summer heat was taking its toll on me. I'd recently been diagnosed with multiple sclerosis, and heat aggravates MS. A debilitating fatigue had kept me under self-imposed house arrest—just my air-conditioner, big-screen TV, dogs, and me—day in and day out, the entire summer. I was bored, lonely, and depressed. My whole life depressed me. On top of feeling lousy and being unable to do the activities I normally enjoyed, I had been forced to give up a high-power executive position and, along with it, my company car.

I thought about going to the air-conditioned mall but nixed that idea. My closets and several bureaus were already stuffed to the max. The thought of my designer suits getting lumps on the shoulders from hangers, the dust on my silk blouses, and the array of matching shoes, purses, and accessories, painful reminders of who I used to be, just colored my mood a darker shade of blue. I certainly didn't need to wear Gucci anything to the supermarket. Besides, I had already attempted to shop through my depression on the Internet. I counted fifty-three purses, dozens of pairs of shoes, and a host of other things I didn't really need. What I needed was to get out of the house.

So, I got into my brand-new red Mustang convertible (also purchased online) and just started driving. Of course, because of the heat, I couldn't even put down the top on my fabulous new convertible. With the air-conditioning blasting, I drove around town and out of town, going nowhere in particular. I passed a sign that said "Indoor Flea Market" and, figuring the building would be air-conditioned, decided to turn around and check it out. I'd never been to a flea market—had never purchased anything that wasn't new, wasn't a brand name, and didn't have at least a double-digit price tag. So, there was no temptation of adding to my overstocked wardrobe, or to my house, for that matter, and a flea market seemed like a safe way to distract me from my boredom and depression.

I felt like an alien who had landed on a different planet—a world lined with tables and tables of junk: an ancient toaster, mismatched dishes, raggedy clothes, and assorted other discards. Why would anyone buy this stuff? Who would have the nerve to sell it? Then I noticed an old man selling used and torn paperback books for a quarter apiece. Clearly, he must need those quarters, I thought. I filled my arms with books and gave him five dollars. His bright smile of thanks was disproportionate to the purchase. My emotions wavered between wonder and depression, but his smile did seem to lift my spirits, if only slightly. I put my books in the car and went back into the flea market.

I walked and looked, as much at the people as at the wares they were buying and selling, fascinated by both the bargain hunters and the peddlers. At one stall, I noticed a little girl's bike with worn pink ribbons—and a $10 price tag—hanging from the handlebars. It looked as if it had been pulled from a Dumpster. I just shook my head and started to move on. Just then, a woman and a little girl stopped to look at the bike. The child was about ten years old, and the pink bows in her long blond pigtails matched the pink ribbons on the bike. Her eyes opened wide with excitement. The woman's face lit up, too, for the briefest second, and she almost smiled, but it quickly passed. She looked to be about my age, yet she seemed twenty years older. Dark circles surrounded her eyes, and her clothes hung loosely on her thin frame, as if held up by the memory of her former figure. The child reached into her pocket and pulled out coins and a few crumpled bills.

"Please, Mommy, please?" she said. "Do I have enough money?"

"Honey, we need so many other things. I don't think there's enough for a bike, too. Let's look for the other stuff we need first, and then we'll see. Okay, sweetie?"

The little girl's face fell, and then a silent under-standing passed between mother and child. She took her mother's hand, and they continued their search for other, more important necessities. My heart was in my throat. I walked up to the man at the booth, prepared to give him a piece of my mind. Why hadn't he sold the bike to the little girl for a dollar or two, or just given it to her? Luckily, I realized the answer before I had the chance to say a word. The seller was an old man dressed in rags, and even though he, too, looked like his heart was in his throat, he clearly needed those ten dollars.

I handed him a ten-dollar bill and asked him to please give the little girl the bike when she and her mother passed by on their way out.

"What's your name, miss, so I can tell the lady who gave her the bike?"

"Just tell her it was a present from a grateful woman."

"Will do," he said. "But do you mind me asking what you're grateful to her for?"

"Everything," I said.

I hid around the corner and watched, half expecting the old guy to just pocket the money. When the mother and daughter approached the table, the vendor flagged them down and wheeled the bike over to the child. The little girl's face glowed, and the mother smiled a full smile that time, tears glistening in her eyes. The mom wrote something down on a piece of paper and gave it to the old man. After they left, I approached the vendor.

"I did as you said, miss, and they were real grateful. She asked me to give this to the anonymous woman," he said, handing me the slip of paper.

The note said that she and her daughter had just moved into town with only the shirts on their backs. She said they were starting a new life here, and I had made their day. She signed her name and wrote down the name of the motel where they were staying temporarily "until we get on our feet."

"Seems like they're running away from something," the vendor said sadly. Or to somewhere, I thought.

When I arrived home, my house no longer seemed like a prison. It seemed comfy and safe, and as luxurious as any five-star hotel. I was as happy to see my dogs as they always are to see me, and I chatted to them happily as I went into the basement and gathered up some boxes. Whistling, I went to my closet and filled the boxes with designer suits and matching shoes and handbags, and pulled piles of clothes from my dresser drawers. I put a note in the box, wishing the mom good luck with her new life and the little girl much joy with her new bike—and thanking them for the gift they'd given me. I wrote that if she had the courage to start over, then so could I.

That miserable hot summer day, I spent ten dollars for a new lease on life. Now, that's what I call a bargain!

—Beth Rothstein Ambler

Heart to Heart

My parents were an unlikely couple. Mother was born and raised in Virginia; Dad was a New York City kid. Her childhood was filled with frilly party dresses and garden tea parties. He played stickball in the streets using the manhole cover as first base. Her parents were professional people, and her education was their number-one priority. His folks were blue-collar workers, who only dreamed of an education beyond high school for their only child. She went on to college and traveled the world, eluding marriage so that she could continue living her dreams. He went on to a union job and learned a trade.

Both found people they cared for and with whom they made plans to share their lives with. She, in fact, became engaged to the son of her father's best friend. The two had grown up together, and their families had always assumed they would one day marry. The engagement was announced with much happiness. Mother and two of her closest friends decided to go to New York City to shop for the bridal trousseau. Her first night in the city, Mother and Dad met at a party.

It was love at first sight, and they spent the entire night talking and sharing their desires for the future. Mother returned to Virginia, gave back her engagement ring, and then moved to New York. She and my father married six months later in a small wedding at city hall. The next year, to their great joy, I was born.

Through the years, my parents often told the story of their fated meeting. And no one who knew the obviously happy couple ever doubted the special love they shared.

My mother's greatest treasure was a small double-hearted copper pin, which Dad had bought for her on their first date, at Coney Island. Her initials were engraved on one heart, his on the other. Mother wore that pin every day. Aside from her wedding band, no other piece of jewelry meant more to her. On several occasions, Dad suggested they replace the little pin with a similar piece made of gold. Mother would not hear of it, saying that it was not a replaceable item. Dad would shake his head and buy her something else.

When my wonderful father died at the tender

age of fifty-nine, my mother went into a deep depression. By then, I was grown and had my own family.
We lived six blocks from my parents. I promised Dad
that I would look after Mom when he was gone, a
promise I wondered how I would keep.

My two young daughters became Mother's
saving grace. She loved them dearly, and the three of
them spent increasingly more time together. Slowly,
Mother found peace and comfort in the family and in
community service. If a charitable organization
needed help, she was there to assist. She became a
member of the American Legion and a volunteer at
one of the area's Veterans' hospitals, and she
received many awards, and personal rewards, for all
the hours she spent with the ill and aging of the
neighborhood. Her life was full, and she appeared to
be happy.

One day, Mother called me at work, saying, in
tears, that she had lost the little copper pin that she
so cherished. We searched the house from top to
bottom. We retraced her steps during the day and
put up reward notices in all the stores. The pin could
not be located, and Mother's depression returned. To
her way of thinking, she had lost my father again,
even though it had been ten years since his death.

Time passed, and Mother again found some comfort in family and in doing for others. Eventually, she
became a great-grandmother, which brought her joy.

But she never forgot about her missing heart pin, and she talked about it constantly.

For her eightieth birthday, we held a special party in my mother's honor. The day was perfect: Mother was surprised; the food was wonderful; the weather was beautiful; and all the children were well behaved. As we gathered up her gifts, she again looked over each present and read every card, as if she didn't want the day to end.

Suddenly, my youngest daughter's little boy came running into the hall. "Nana, Nana," he yelled. "I didn't get to give you my present."

He held out a small box wrapped in aluminum foil.

Mother asked if he had made her something at school.

"No, Nana," he replied. "I was going to paint you a picture in school, and Mommy gave me an old blouse from a box in the attic to use as a smock so I wouldn't get dirty. When I put the blouse over my head, a pin stuck me. It was pretty, so I decided to give it to you for your birthday. I wrapped it all by myself, because I love you."

When Mother opened her great-grandson's gift, her face turned white. We rushed to her, fearing she would faint. She looked up at us, smiling.

"Children," she said, smiling, "I just received my

eightieth birthday present from your father." And she held up the little copper heart pin that had been lost so many years before.

Four years later, I removed the pin from my mother's sweater the day she passed away. And I realized that some hearts can never be parted.

—*Anne Carter*

My Time

She didn't see him. It was dark. He had hidden himself well. She was concentrating on her running form. She didn't hear him. She was focusing on her breathing, the soles of her shoes striking the pavement. She didn't anticipate it. She was anticipating, preparing for, the race to be held that weekend.

When the blow struck her head, Robin felt confusion first—then, an instant later, sheer terror. As if from a distance, she heard her own screams rip through the still air as she crumpled to the ground. Suddenly, a knife was thrust tightly against her throat. In a menacing growl, the attacker warned that if she made another sound, he would kill her. Instinctively, she knew he would. Her will to survive stronger even than this brutal attack, she stayed silent, she stayed conscious, she endured.

After the assault, he yanked her rings from her fingers and her watch from her wrist. She noticed the time. In ten long minutes, in just ten minutes, her life had passed before her, was torn from her, it seemed. Yet, she was still alive. He was still holding her down. And still, she remained silent and motionless, alert yet apart from her body. He removed the knife from her throat, and before she could take another breath, he punched her in the face with such force that it broke her nose and knocked her into semiconsciousness. Then the brute, the coward, ran away.

For a few minutes she was too afraid to move. Her mind raced as she tried to shake off the pain and the disorientation, to comprehend what had happened. Then she sobbed, partly in horror, partly in relief that she was still alive. Fear and revulsion, gratitude and outrage, a jumble of intense emotions hit her all at once, temporarily paralyzing her, keeping her pinned to the ground. Finally, slowly she rose and stumbled numbly to safety.

She did not feel safe. She did not feel like herself. She didn't trust men, didn't dare trust men. And she did not run.

Running had been one of Robin's greatest joys. After the attack, she couldn't imagine ever running again. She rarely even left her house. The police were never able to arrest or even to identify her assailant. He was still out there. He could do it again.

If not him, then some other assailant could be just around the next corner, waiting to jump out and take so much more than a watch, a ring, so much more than ten hellish minutes of a life. Hers had been spared, but her freedom to run, her sense of well-being, her sense of self, had been destroyed.

Weeks went by. Recurring flashbacks of the attack haunted her days; nightmares tortured her sleep. She ventured out of her house only when necessary, only in daylight, and always with dread, acutely aware of the dangers lurking in the shadows. She found it exceedingly difficult to relate to men, even those she'd known long and trusted implicitly before the assault. What were they really like, she wondered, when no one was watching? Her running shoes were shoved out of sight, banishing the last semblance of the person she no longer was and would never be again. That is what she told herself. That is what she believed.

But it was not, she realized one morning, what she wanted. Robin had awakened early that day, and for the first time in a long while, she felt a glimmer of hope stir deep inside. She realized that she wanted to feel joy again. She wanted her life back. She wanted it desperately. But she didn't know how to get it. No answer came that morning.

But that night she dreamed—and for once, it was not a nightmare. The dream was peaceful and, oddly, she thought, very detailed. In her dream, she saw a huge clock with all twenty-four hours, rather than the customary twelve, displayed on its face. All the minutes were also showing, and quite prominently. At the bottom of the clock, the number "1440" flashed. For some reason, the dream comforted Robin.

The next morning, Robin remembered the dream. For the first time since the attack, she started her day off thinking about something other than the assault. Instead, she thought about the giant twenty-four-hour clock. Why was she dreaming about a clock? Why did the minutes on the clock seem so important? What did that flashing number represent, and why was it flashing? All morning she was preoccupied with the dream. Then, on an impulse, she pulled out her calculator and multiplied 24 (hours) by 60 (minutes): The total was 1,440! So, that's what it was—the number of minutes in a day! Robin wondered how many minutes were in a week and a month; then she calculated the number of minutes in a year. She sat and stared at the number: 525,600— more than half a million minutes. If she lived to be eighty . . . she wondered and calculated . . . Wow! Almost 30 million more minutes!

Then, it struck her like a melodious chime on a fine clock. Robin suddenly realized that she had been spending every waking minute of every day and many nightmarish minutes of every night reliving one ten-minute, if horrific, experience. It occurred to her that she still had tens of millions of minutes yet to live. And it was her choice how she would spend them. She put down the calculator and got out her running shoes. That day, Robin ran. And she ran the next day . . . and the next . . . and the next.

She also joined a support group for women who had been assaulted or battered. From those counseling sessions, she learned that all of the women who were healing from their trauma shared one thing in common: Each had experienced a sudden realization that it was up to them to put down the heavy load they'd been carrying and to pick up their shattered lives and rebuild them. For Robin, that moment of clarity came from a dream about the 1,440 minutes in a day. From that moment on, she was determined to live the remaining millions of minutes of her life fully and free of fear.

The day I attended the therapy group and heard Robin share her empowering story, I realized that I, too, had a choice, and I made one. I chose not to spend another moment on the past—and to celebrate the precious moments of my life every day.

—*Lynn Seely*

Joan's Lover

As Joan found her twentieth wedding anniversary approaching, she also found herself with an unfulfilled desire. Despite a happy marriage and six beautiful children, something was missing. She had an itch to experience something beyond the usual rhythm of her daily life. So it was that when her youngest child was about to go off to kindergarten, something happened that touched Joan's soul and changed her forever: A "lover" stepped into her life.

He was tall, dark, and handsome, a big fellow from out West. Lank and lean, he had a thick neck, sinewy muscles, and a sure stride. At the time, he needed Joan as much as she needed him. They both had obstacles to overcome. His were from years of hard living; hers were more serious. For both, they were health related.

Since childhood, Joan had suffered with eye problems. A progressively deteriorating condition called Steven Johnson syndrome had taken hold, and Joan could no longer drive or perform routine tasks without great difficulty. Each day, she suffered the pain and frustration of not only losing her eyesight, but also of losing her independence. Her new lover seemed to sense her problem right from the start and showed uncommon compassion and kindness. They shared a synergy that comes along only once in a lifetime. And when it does, it knows no bounds.

From the start, the pair knew they had something in common and special. Each had a love of being outdoors and experiencing the wonders of nature. They began going for long walks in the woods, delighting in the leaves crackling beneath their feet and the exhilaration of fresh air in their nostrils. Without a word, each seemed to sense the other's next move. Together they discovered a whole new world, one that included independence, self-esteem, and, most of all, fun. He became her eyes, and through him she saw life from a new vantage point. When he was around, she felt like she was sitting on top of the world.

He was a real gentleman. Joan's friends said he had class and really knew how to treat a woman. On walks, he compensated for her unsure steps. He always made her feel safe, especially when her neck was affectionately nuzzled against his. As time passed, the pair began to travel together. Complete strangers could see their compatibility and the comfort they drew from each other.

Joan began spending more and more time with her lover, and her family saw a new side of her. Self-confidence emerged, and happiness radiated from her. She became a better wife and mother because of the big, handsome guy she called Lover. But he was not the type of lover who would break up a marriage or steal away a wife or mother. This lover only enhanced and enriched her other relationships. He was a giver, and he was thankful for every little gesture of kindness bestowed upon him. A pat on his back, a stroke of his neck were met with gratitude and appreciation. So, with her husband's blessing and encouragement, Joan continued her liaison for many wonderful years.

Joan and her lover had a commitment to each other and to their mutual quest for new experiences and adventures. These adventures took place on trails, in woods, in stables and paddocks. These were the places where Lover felt most comfortable, because he was an outdoorsman at heart, raised on a farm. No one ever knew his birth name. Everyone just called him Joan's Lover, a name suited to his nature and special qualities.

And he was special, a real gift. He had been an

anniversary present to Joan from her husband, Tom, who also sensed her longing for something more than the sometimes mundane maneuvers of marriage and motherhood. Indeed, she got more than she could have expected on that warm August day when a trailer showed up at her old farmhouse and out stepped the beautiful five-year-old Thoroughbred named Lover.

For twenty-five years, Joan and Lover were together, each learning from the other. In the beginning, with brushing and grooming, they got acquainted with each other. Then they began going on short trail rides. Soon they were fox hunting, jumping fences, and competing in dressage riding. When Joan could no longer keep up with those activities, Lover was content just to be by her side or under her seat. In dangerous situations, he took his place between Joan and other horses. As her sight grew worse and her eyes became a constant source of pain, Lover sensed it and soothed her. He was always there for her.

Not so on a cold day in November, when Lover, who was by then nearly thirty years old, got sick. Now, even their love and determination could not conquer the severe colic festering in his stomach. This time, he needed his Joan like she had always needed him. She knew he was in pain and that the best thing for him was to put him down.

But it was not going to be easy. After all, Joan and Lover were a team. They had always done everything together, and this last journey would be no different from the rest. So, as usual, Joan went to Lover's stall and stroked him, and spoke softly to him. When she began leading him out, he thought he was going to graze on some grass on the edge of their favorite spot, the woods behind his stable. Joan stood next to his side and watched as the veterinarian injected Lover with the drug that would put that big, wonderful heart to sleep forever. As he slipped into unconsciousness, Joan rested her head on him for comfort, just as she had done so many times in their long courtship. Only this time, Joan's partner no longer snorted jubilant bursts of warm air or threw back his self-assured head as if to say, "I love you, too." He was silent, and still.

But Lover's memory is still very much alive, and his spirit continues to bring her love and joy. He is buried under a big beautiful spruce on the edge of the woods in back of Joan's house. Every day when she goes to that tree to pray, she is reminded of the beauty of nature and of all God's gifts of creation, especially a horse named Lover.

—*Sharon Hazard*

A New Year's Magic

New Year's Eve has always been a magical time to me. I like the revelry—the champagne and fancy dresses, the noisemakers and streamers. Celebrating the passing year and ringing in the next remind me that time is short and life is precious.

As a child I always spent New Year's Eve night with my grandparents. I could never stay awake until midnight, but I can still feel my grandmother's warm hands gently shaking me awake as she whispered, "The ball will be dropping soon." Then, the three of us would watch with wonder as the glittering ball made its descent—ten, nine, eight, seven, six, five, four, three, two, one! And we'd cheer as the crowd erupted in celebration!

When I matured, I began spending New Year's Eve with friends, but I always phoned my grandparents just after midnight. "Did you watch the ball drop?" we'd ask one another. Inevitably, of course, the answer was always, "Yes!" Then, we'd wish each other a Happy New Year and send our love over the phone line. I repeated this ritual every year until they were both gone.

In my early twenties, I became obsessed with going to New York City to watch the countdown live at Times Square. I have propositioned most of my family and close friends with dinner at an elegant restaurant, dancing at a fancy hotel, and the mad dash at eleven o'clock to join the crowd assembled under the ball. So far, there have been no takers. So, year after year, I continue to watch the revelers on television, promising myself that one day I will be among them, even if I have to go alone.

This year, 2002, was a most solemn New Year's. Everyone I know stayed home and seemed uninterested in marking the holiday with anything more than a quiet meal and a bottle of wine. My husband's sole interest was in watching every minute of a Philadelphia Eagles playoff game. He agreed to take our two young daughters and me to an early dinner as long as we returned in time for the kickoff. No lingering over dessert for us. But it was better than no celebration, so the four of us went out to dinner and enjoyed it. Besides, there would be time for champagne and romance after the game. Since I know things seldom work as planned, I didn't dare play coy with my husband or just hint.

"When the game is over, I want you to spend time with me," I told him. He promised to be "all mine," but still I felt upset. "You know how much this night means to me," I whined, trying to seal the deal. He nodded. I was not reassured.

Maybe it was the full dinner, the excitement of the game, the lull of a quiet house, or that he was just plain tired. Whatever the reason, my husband fell asleep shortly after our children did, and I found myself alone on my favorite holiday. Filled with disappointment, I paced the house, tried in vain to read a paperback, and made hot chocolate. Finally, I settled into a chair in front of a dying fire; it gave off little warmth.

At 11:00, I added a few logs to the hearth and dimmed the lights, transforming the room into a warm, sensuous sanctum. I turned on the Christmas tree lights, opened a bottle of champagne, and filled two crystal flutes.

"The ball's dropping soon," I said, gently shaking my husband. He rose up on one elbow to sip the champagne, murmured "Happy New Year," and returned to his peaceful slumber.

For the first time in my life, I watched the ball drop alone. The longing to call my grandparents became a physical ache, and I envied the people at

Times Square more than ever. I felt like an interloper as I searched their joyful faces. I tried to command from memory the ghosts of past New Year's Eves: of my grandfather and me banging pots on his front porch, of my mother in a sparkling silver gown, of cinnamon kisses from a handsome boy at midnight. But the house remained silent as I blinked a lone tear from my eye.

I turned off the television and went to kiss each of my daughters in their beds, whispering "I love you" into their soft hair. I thought of waking them, bundling them up, and taking them outside to bang tin bowls with wooden spoons. Instead, I tucked the blankets around my four-year-old, sleeping peacefully in her bed, and around my youngest, content in her crib. I hugged my dog, perhaps tighter than he liked. Then I went downstairs to turn off the lights and snuff out the fire.

The fragrant evergreen seemed to shimmer in the soft glow of the fireplace embers, and its colored lights reflected in the picture window. I felt both elated and depressed in my solitary observance of such beauty. I went to the window and looked out at the quiet night. As I watched the prism of colored lights dance over the snow-blanketed lawn, I sipped champagne and smiled. How could I have failed to notice that my front lawn resembled a rainbow sorbet?

I heard them before I saw them. They were singing *Auld Lang Syne*, laughing as they struggled to recall the words. There were two girls and four boys, strolling along the sidewalk, oblivious to the bitter wind and lateness of hour. They reminded me of past New Year's Eves and youthful pleasures. I liked them immediately.

"Virgin snow!" the tall one in the royal blue scarf called, as he dove and rolled on my front lawn.

"I wonder if we can make colored snowballs with it?" said the girl in the black ski coat.

She stood just under my window, and I stepped back into the curtains so as not to startle her. She dipped into a patch of pink powder and fired it at the loud boy with the tasseled hat. She missed, but he chased her anyway, giving her a gentleman's version of a whitewash.

I observed them with secret glee as they demolished my pristine snow. A part of me longed to throw on my old blue parka and join them, but mostly I felt content to just watch. Their joyous presence lifted the shadow of loneliness from my soul. I pressed closer to the window, touched the cool glass with my fingertips.

"I'm so glad you chose my snow," I whispered to them.

Just then the phone rang. It was my cousin, a grown man and expectant father with whom I've shared a strong bond since childhood. I hadn't expected to hear from him and was touched by his call. He was having a party and had to shout to be heard over the dance music and merrymaking.

"Happy New Year, cousin!" he said. "Are you having a good time?"

"Great, just great," I answered.

"It sounds quiet there. Are you alone?" he asked.

I looked out at my snow angels, pictured my family warm and safe in their beds, and held my cousin's handsome face for a moment in my mind's eye.

"No, I'm not alone," I said. "Happy New Year to you, too!"

—Christine Caldwell

The Mended Cup

I was a little anxious about how Maggie would receive the gift. It was, after all, old and used and in less-than-pristine condition.

Maggie Mae, my granddaughter, was moving out of her parents' home and into her first apartment. She had come by to pick up Grandma's contributions to her new furnishings. She untied the bow, unwrapped the violet crepe paper, and stared down at the gold trim of an antique cup.

"Grandma, it's beautiful," she said as she lifted it from the packaging. Then, seeing the cracks in the base and the handle glued on with epoxy, she added, "But . . . this cup is broken."

"No, honey, it is mended," I said. And then I told her about the cup's history.

That cup was given to me long before you were born by one of my dearest friends, Dianne. Remember when you and I used to play tea party when you were little? Well, my friend and I would share tea times just like that. We'd get together often, to talk over tea about all the joys and challenges that life had presented us with. We always set a lovely table with fine china and embroidered napkins and home-baked cookies. That teacup has heard many interesting stories and more than a few secrets. Many teardrops have mixed with the tea and cream and sugar in that cup. Why, the very day you were born, we celebrated the joy and excitement with our special teatime.

In those days, women rarely went to therapists and psychologists with their problems. They went to one another. My friend Dianne lived just up the street. There were many mornings when I would run up to her house in my robe and slippers, and we'd sit by the fireside and sip our tea. When I had a problem, Dianne would listen and comfort me. And she would come to me in the same way. We were each other's confidantes and counselors, but more than that, we were friends.

Dianne and I both loved pretty things and looked forward to setting our teacart with fresh flowers and fine china. Our worlds ran parallel in many other areas as well. When she got divorced, so did I. When she lost a loved one, the same would take place in my life. We were constantly comforting and being comforted by each other. I'd show up at her door, or she would show up at mine, cup in hand, and then the healing process of talking and listening, of sharing and supporting, would begin.

It wasn't always a crisis. Sometimes—actually, most of the time—we would sit in pleasant company and discuss the color of wallpaper, where to hang a picture, and girly things, like makeup and hairstyles. I remember how excited I was when I bought a gorgeous dress for my class reunion. I couldn't wait to show her, and, of course, she offered to lend just the right piece of her jewelry to complement it.

Men were always a popular topic. When we were single, we'd compare notes on the men in our lives and on the attributes of the ideal partner. We could go through a gallon of tea on those nights, discussing all the toads we had kissed before we found our princes.

On summer nights we took our tea out on the patio with lit candles and fresh flowers, discussing life and the pursuit of happiness. We sipped as the seasons—and our lives—changed. When we were confused, after one of our teatimes everything seemed to make sense, if only for the time it took to brew and enjoy our tea together. As I look back on those many years, I can barely recall most of the heartbreaks and headaches that sent me shuffling off to Dianne's in my slippers, teacup in hand. But, I remember vividly every one of our teatimes, and treasure those memories.

Eventually, Dianne moved away, but I kept my teacup and would think of her whenever I used it. Then I sold my house, and while packing, I dropped my special cup. I did the best I could to put it all back together. The cup was never the same, but I realized that it really didn't matter. Even though it no longer holds liquid, it is filled to the brim with the sweet memories of years gone by.

And so, I would like you to have it.

"Thank you, Grandma," Maggie said after a short silence.

And when, as we hugged good-bye, Maggie invited me over to her new place for tea the next day, I knew that my special teacup was in good hands—and that it was the perfect gift for a grand-daughter starting out on her own journey.

—*Barbara Rich*

# Emily's Front Porch

We met several years ago when we were both cast in a play at the local community theater. We exchanged pleasantries at rehearsals and worked well together on scenes in which we both appeared. Then, one night she invited everyone over to her house for a get-together after rehearsal. I walked in the door, made some wisecrack that only she laughed at, and we have been the best of friends ever since.

It has never mattered that Emily was graduating from high school the year I was born. Nor did it matter that we came from completely different backgrounds. It made no difference that she was married with grown children, and that I was footloose and fancy-free. It never seemed odd that as she stayed at home caring for her husband and family, I pursued a prestigious marketing career. We were friends in a way that only women who have found a soul sister can understand.

We would sit for hours on her front porch, sipping wine and discussing books, theater, and relationships, and solving all the world's problems. She supported me through a challenging romance with the man who is now my husband, and she was the matron of honor at our wedding. I was there for her when her husband decided that the grass was greener with another woman, and when she was thinking of going back to school, I told her I believed in her. With her encouragement ringing in my soul, I launched my own successful consulting business.

Emily returned to school and became a teacher. Although she couldn't be with me in body, I know that she was with me in spirit the day I gave birth to my son. And when being with Wyatt seemed more important than being at work, she supported my decision to put career aside for a while and to be a stay-at-home mom. Through career changes, marriage and divorce, births and deaths, good times and bad, our friendship sustained us through it all.

Then my husband was transferred halfway across the country.

Her front porch had been the calm in all the storms of my life. It was the place I would go to celebrate my successes and mourn my losses. Now, her front porch would be 2,000 miles away.

As we always did, we made the best of it. We had hour-long phone calls during which we would each get a glass of wine and sit on our respective front porches to talk. It was the next best thing to being there. We wrote pages and pages of letters back and forth, and every time I received one from her, I felt like laughing and crying at the same time. But it wasn't the same.

Finally, last fall I got the opportunity to go on what I have termed a "pilgrimage" back to the South. Because my husband was unable to get any extended time off from work, I took the baby to visit every friend and relative we had south of the Mason-Dixon line. Any trip with an infant is challenging, but day after day of hour after hour in a car, interspersed with him being pinched, poked, and prodded by strangers, made for a trying experience for both of us. Different food, water, and beds each night didn't help. The thing that kept me going was the knowledge that I would get to spend the last night at Emily's.

After two weeks of travel, her front porch was finally in sight. It had never looked so good, nor had the wine been so cold or the conversation so warm as it was that evening. Wyatt adored her, sensing, I believe, that we were in the presence of someone I loved and trusted a great deal, and someone who loved and trusted me. It also seemed like he knew we needed some quiet time for real girl talk. He ate a huge dinner, downed a sippy cup of milk, and dozed off earlier than usual. I put him down in his Pack 'N Play in the back bedroom and returned to the porch.

Soon after, Emily's twenty-two-year-old daughter, Marilyn, arrived home after her evening shift at the restaurant where she waited tables. After hugs and kisses, she said she was exhausted and went to lie down. Emily and I continued to gab as if we hadn't spoken in years.

It must have been close to an hour later that I said, "I'd better go check on Wyatt." Apparently, my comment reminded Emily that we had put Wyatt to bed in Marilyn's room. We jumped up, not in a panic, but both wondering how these two diverse souls were coexisting.

We quietly opened the door to Marilyn's darkened bedroom, and I tiptoed over to the Pack 'N Play. He wasn't there. Okay, now I was starting to panic. But just as my heart began to palpitate, Emily motioned for me to look at the bed. In the half-light from a small lamp on the bedside table, I could just make out Marilyn's sleeping silhouette, and snuggled up next to her was my Wyatt. She had her arms around him, and they were both breathing softly, their noses almost touching, they were so close.

There we stood, shoulder to shoulder, watching our "babies" sleeping peacefully together. In that moment it seemed as if our entire relationship had come full circle. We had been through so much together over the years, and yet for those few minutes, nothing existed outside of that room. I breathed a great sigh and knew that no matter how far away I lived, I could summon up that beautiful experience in my mind and would again know the comfort of being back on Emily's front porch.

—*Lauren Cassel Brownell*

A Gift of New Beginnings

I had my first notions of taking early retirement about a year ago. These thoughts invaded my consciousness like a magpie, prattling on incessantly until I could no longer deny the significance and reality of the message.

As a female executive for more than thirty years, my career has been fraught with the usual debilitating impacts of stress and political agendas. I spent more than twenty of those years in the financial sector, an industry in which men traditionally reign. Staying alive has often been a tough survival game, challenged by disconnects in gender communication and my inability to engage in deal making at the urinal.

Despite the difficulties, I survived, and I loved working. I *was* my job. Why, then, was I thinking of retirement at fifty-two years old? The concept intrigued and unnerved me in alternating moments of confusion, excitement, and panic over the months to follow. I had no role model to guide me. My husband had been downsized and forced into retirement the year before, and he was devastated by the whole humiliating process. He hadn't been ready for it, and he was terrified. As I watched him go through this, I witnessed the pain he suffered in losing his identity, his salary, and his dignity. He was still adjusting.

My friends couldn't help me. They were all working and building their nest eggs for that well-planned retirement, sometime in the future. The television commercials reminded me that freedom comes only at fifty-five, if at all. My financial planner and my retirement savings plan portfolio confirmed that I had not yet come of age.

My retirement thoughts persisted, although I was afraid to listen. Who would I be without my business card? How could I give up the money, the bonuses, the stock options? But the internal nudging continued to taunt me with the many things I wanted to pursue, especially my passion for writing. I felt time running out.

There were other realities to consider: the chronic exhaustion that came from keeping up with the demands of the job, and the fear that my lupus condition would activate and force me to retire the hard way. If I waited much longer, would the exhaustion or lupus prevent me from pursuing those interests I'd pushed aside as I fought my way up the corporate ladder?

The year passed, and I finally cut the umbilical cord and announced my plans to retire. With a healthy mix of shock and envy, my colleagues queried me with cautious looks and a desperate need to rationalize my decision. They asked whether I had been downsized or was just downright mad.

At first, I would occasionally wake in the middle of the night with heart palpitations. But, when the sun came up in the morning, there was always a feeling of "rightness" in my decision. It was time to break the breathless pace of my life and pass on the leadership baton to my fleet of able recruits. I felt an almost magical beckoning to the adventure ahead.

I have never liked the image that goes with retirement, partly because I don't play golf and have no plans to move to Florida. I've always found comfort in words, so I turned to the dictionary. There, I found such depressing definitions of retirement as "seclusion" and "hibernation." My handy thesaurus was no better, with synonyms like "being put out to pasture" and "to go out of circulation." That was the opposite of what I sought from retirement. My book of antonyms saved me, with its citation of "arrive" as the opposite of "retire." To arrive was "to reach a destination or place," "to attain success or fame," "a coming to anything as a result of effort, action, or natural process." That was more like it. That was for me.

So, armed with a sense of pioneering spirit, I looked forward to my "arrivement." I am now several months into my new life. My early-morning walks, free of voice mail, e-mail, and cell phones, energize me. The days seem longer now, and yet richer, because each precious minute belongs to me. I listen as the waves pound a rhythm into the sand on the shore. I experience the explosion of spring for the first time since childhood. I get massages and take long, luxurious baths. I visit an elderly neighbor and bring him flowers. And I record my days, spent exactly as I choose to, in a journal.

I read books, burying myself in the classics I've neglected for so long. I make travel plans and look forward to the people and places I'll visit in the days ahead. I breathe deeply and meditate. I spend time with my daughter, my husband, and my two wonderful sisters. And I write, dusting off the cleansing words that arise in this cycle of renewal, carrying me forward in this chariot I've given myself, this gift of new beginnings.

—Pat Skene

The Moon, Two Stars, and Italy

I have gotten a lot out of being a mother: pleasure, pride, white hair, sleepless nights. I've also gotten the moon, two stars, and Italy. The moon is a pin, and the two stars are earrings, presented to me in a blue Tiffany box by my daughter, Meg, a Christmas gift marking her first adult job (and the first year she didn't have to borrow money from me to buy her presents).

Italy takes a little more explaining. Meg fell in love with Italy while studying there one summer. On a student budget, she couldn't buy art books to bring home, but the stories she told painted beautiful pictures. And the meals! Crisp bruschetta, tangy tomatoes. When I sighed over her descriptions of the Botticelli paintings in the Uffizi Gallery, she said, "I know you'd love Italy, Mom. We should go there together next year."

A long time passed after she made that suggestion. Meanwhile, Meg and I had gone through the usual turmoil that parents and children seem to experience when a child is becoming an adult. The points of connection between us, once so thick and fast, had stretched thin over time. Living 3,000 miles apart didn't make it any easier. Though I wanted to go to Italy with Meg, the chance to take her up on her offer never seemed to arrive. We were too busy navigating life's detours. If it wasn't my leaving a downtown job to write, it was her graduation from law school. She got married. We remodeled our home. Meg moved to New York to start her career. I enrolled in training for the volunteer programs I'd had no time for in the past.

Italy began to look like a place my husband and I would visit after he retired. Then one Christmas Meg said, "I have vacation time I need to use up this spring and no plans. What about that trip to Italy? I don't suppose you're free, are you?"

I was.

Florence was first. Meg arranged for us to stay at the convent where she'd lived as a student. My tall, confident, dark-haired daughter strode through the quiet halls to our room, oblivious to surroundings she'd seen many times before. I followed, rubber-necking at all the paintings, statues, and old furniture. When I opened the door to our room, she was standing next to the window, smiling. The window was cut into a white-plastered, thirteenth-century wall and draped in soft, gauzy curtains that drifted lazily from ceiling to floor. Through the window I saw, close to the convent, an olive grove with new leaves about to burst out. In the far distance, a line of dark trees, as slender and elegant as Prada models, formed a crest on the green hills. Between the two sets of trees, Florence's cathedral rose from the surrounding terra-cotta rooftops, its dome thrusting toward the sky, daring the earth to pull it back.

"Better than the movie *A Room with a View,* isn't it?" Meg said.

The next morning we were drawn to the dining room by the yeasty smell of baking bread overlaid with the rich aroma of brewing coffee. We smeared our crusty rolls with sweet butter and strawberry jam, gulped the strong black coffee, and planned our day. Meg knew which museums to visit early and which to swing by at the end of the day. She knew how to find a cheap lunch. With her recon information, we plotted our course as carefully as any general made battle plans.

At the end of the day, footsore and overdosed on Renaissance art, we collapsed into wrought iron chairs at an outdoor café. When the carafe of wine and plate of *antipasti* arrived, we sipped Tuscan red wine and munched tiny slices of bread topped with tomatoes, basil, and olive oil. And we began to talk.

That first day we talked about art and architecture, about sculpture and painting, each of us surprising the other by what we knew—and sometimes by what we didn't know. When we finished Meg's list in Florence, we saw Siena, San Gimignano, and Fiesole. One cloudy, misty morning, we left our convent before even the nuns were up and boarded the train. The sun broke through just as we walked out of the train station in Venice. We took our afternoon wine and *antipasti* in a small restaurant fronting a canal, just before catching the train back to Florence.

By Venice, we had begun to talk about more than just what we'd seen that day. We moved on to other things, to subjects that hadn't made it into the cards and letters we'd exchanged over the eight years she'd lived in Washington, D.C., and I had lived in Portland, Oregon. We mentioned things we'd somehow forgotten to say in phone conversations, such as where we were buying our clothes these days. We discussed things that give depth and shadings to relationships, such as new books and movies that we liked. We shared things that seem important enough to talk about only in person but seem inappropriate for a discussion over Christmas dinner, such as my problems with an aging mother and an alcoholic brother.

We discovered that both of us thought it was fun

to ride in a sport utility vehicle but would never own one. She asked what I wanted to be called when she and her husband had children. We talked about my arrangements for retirement and her plans for her career before and after motherhood.

Gradually, as we sat and sipped and watched the world walk by, we caught up with each other's lives. By the time we got to Rome, we were in a groove. On our first afternoon we went to the Piazza Navonne, Meg's favorite of all of Rome's many outdoor squares, and watched kids splash about in the fountain. The next day, for our cocktail hour, she consulted our map, walked us around several blocks, and finally found the street she wanted, one that brought us into a piazza at the best angle for a perfect view of the Pantheon. We found a café, sat down, and watched as truckloads of chairs were brought in for Palm Sunday services.

The Pantheon had been a place of worship for more than three thousand years, as it would be that Sunday. On our day in St. Peter's Cathedral, I listened to the sounds of tennis-shoed tourists mingle with centuries of whispered prayers while I searched for Michelangelo's statue of Mary and Jesus, his *Pietà*. Meg was more intent on fulfilling a mission than on seeing statuary. She'd been charged with acquiring holy water for her mother-in-law but wasn't sure how to go about it. Perhaps, she said, a simple "dip and run" would accomplish the task. No, I said, too tacky. Fortunately, an English-speaking Italian priest took pity on us. After he told us he liked Pepsi to prove he could speak our language, he herded us into the sacristy where a platoon of priests robed for mass. At his direction one of them filled a bottle with holy water for the "young lady's mother-in-law in New Jersey." We never knew why he thought Meg's mother-in-law lived in New Jersey.

Each day we explored small streets near our hotel, picking out a little *trattoria* for dinner or finding yet another church to visit. Thanks to a chocolate shop—which we smelled long before we saw it—we found out about the huge chocolate eggs wrapped in pastel cellophane that Italians give as Easter gifts. We bought a few smaller eggs to take home as presents, ate them in our hotel room, bought a few more, and ate them, too.

On our last full day we visited the ruins of ancient Rome. It was Palm Sunday, and because of a procession marking the holy day, there were no cars on the street. Free of the infamous Roman traffic, we walked around the Colosseum, recited what we could remember of Marc Antony's "friends, Romans, countrymen" speech at the appropriate place in the Forum, and struggled, using my rusty Latin, to translate ancient words carved in stone.

Two weeks slipped by quickly. On the plane

home we laughed about the funny things we'd found out about each other during our trip: Meg's fondness for fountains. Mine for signs. Meg's door fetish. My unexpected desire to see the Baptistery doors in Florence rather than Michelangelo's *David*. Between us we had taken seven rolls of photos, sent home three boxes of pottery, and collected innumerable stories about piazzas, pizza, and pickpockets. We'd also bought many gifts. The customs form I filled out listed Easter candy, art books, Florentine paper, olive oil, and silk ties. But U.S. law doesn't ask for an accounting of the most valuable gifts I brought back from that trip.

Meg helped me to see an Old-World culture through my New-World eyes. Gradually, over our two weeks together, we both began to see an old relationship, mother and child, with new insights. Without losing the daughter I had always loved, I began to see the woman she was becoming. She found the outline of the woman I have always been, hidden in her mother. My daughter gave me the moon, two stars, and Italy. And Italy showed us the moon, the stars, and the universe in each other. No gift could be more precious.

—*Peggy Bird*

Chrysalis

The matchbook, a memento from my solitary retreat at Cradle Mountain Lodge, nearly leaps out of my hand as the memory associated with it seeps into my mind, spreading its heat over my neurons. Feelings I haven't experienced for nearly three years suddenly rise to the surface. And I remember . . .

I had chosen a remote place to get away from it all—from my job and family and him. But mostly, I needed to get back to the self I had lost in his insecurities and in my insecurity with him.

It had taken all my strength to get out of the relationship, which had stifled me and had taken so much out of me. Yet, afterward, I felt hollow and displaced, lost and raw. Everywhere I turned, I was reminded of the life we'd shared and the unfamiliarity of life alone.

How does one go from two to one, from us to me? Had there ever been a "me" in our marriage?

My therapist had suggested a "find me" holiday. I figured what better place than halfway around the world in Tasmania.

The lodge at Cradle Mountain was a beautiful two-story log structure with a steeply gabled roof and a massive porch. A mist hung over the woods, masking the peak of the mountain. The pine-scented air was so crisp and clean it almost hurt. My immediate thought was, I think I like this place.

My cabin was nestled amongst the trees, barely visible from the road. Freshly chopped wood was stacked near the entrance. Inside, a striking fireplace stood guard over the bedroom, and the tiny kitchen was stocked with everything one could possibly need. A small porch overlooked a narrow creek and a slim yard alive with two small wallabies and a wombat. I was enthralled.

I had never vacationed alone, and found it to be an uncomfortable and yet strangely comforting experience. Despite the pleasant environment, I didn't know quite what to do.

"Well, old girl," I finally said to myself. "If you're going to go it alone, you might as well do it up right. Let's see . . . shall I break open some wine? How about some Brie and crackers?

"Yes, you say? Okay, then, we've got the makings

of a wonderful evening here.

"A fire would be wonderful. Do you remember how to make a fire?

"Vaguely," I answered, glad that my therapist couldn't hear me not only talking to myself, but also answering.

I felt a sense of pride when, after delving into my early Girl Scout training, I managed to start a fire, sooner than I had expected and with only three matches.

Soon, the fire licked the logs, teasing them into consumption. Heat radiated outward like ripples on a pond, wrapping me in a cozy warm blanket. I sank farther into the overstuffed chair, becoming almost one with it, and then noticed it was snowing. Through the window I watched as huge flakes gently floated to and fro before resting on any horizontal surface. The wine caught the light and reflected red splashes of tentacled color on the wall, mesmerizing me. As the wine's tannic acid played with my tongue and wove its way to my stomach, a glow began to spread through my body, finally filling my brain. I had never before known such peace, such contentment.

Then, on the wall lit by the fire's flickering light, I watched as myriad scenes began to play before my eyes, as though a movie of my life were being presented to me. I could not turn my eyes away. I wondered hazily, "Am I awake or asleep?" but had no answer, nor did I care. The show began with images from my childhood, of me being teased and of me teasing another child. Both children began to cry, and I could feel the pain, both my own and my companion's, in the way that a child whose delicate flesh is suddenly sliced might feel, but now doubled with the awareness of having caused pain.

The display continued, playing out events of my past, some of which I was proud, perhaps too proud, and some I regretted. As the reel spun, the wound inside me seemed to widen. Then, my marriage and its slow decay paraded before me. The protective shell I'd hovered behind melted away, and my sorrow spilled out like oil from a leaky tanker. Tears from deep within my soul, so long dammed up within me, sprang forth with force. I cried and cried, hard, racking sobs, for what seemed an eternity, certain I could not survive such pain.

Through blurry eyes, I saw the pictures begin to change. The children, though still teasing, hugged each other and walked away, hand in hand. The proud moments seemed more humble, the behavior more tolerable. It was as if the Divine had given me an opportunity to rearrange the scenes to my liking, to rewrite my parts of the script, to play it over and over until it felt right.

With this newly scripted vision of my life, I could

see clearly the situations that had led to my divorce, including my previously unrecognized part in it. With each clarified and revised scene, the hurt and burden that had been weighing me down diminished. The harsh sobs calmed to cleansing weeping, and then to gentle tears slipping silently down my cheeks. My head and shoulders, for so long hunched over in remorse and despair, began to lift and to straighten as I shed the load of my past.

Suddenly, an acute awareness of my surroundings startled me from my reverie. It was as if I had left the room—indeed, left this world—and had just returned. I was still sitting in the big chair, and the wineglass still dangled in my fingers, unspilled and unfinished. The fire had died to glowing embers, with only the occasional flicker of flame. Outside, there were several inches of freshly fallen snow, and the night sky had begun its waning to dawn. Yet, I had no sense or memory of having fallen asleep or waking.

A chill raised goosebumps on my arms, whether from the cold or from my new sense of awareness, I was uncertain. I felt as renewed as my snow-blanketed surroundings, yet as wise as an old sage; as fragile as a snowflake, yet as tough as steel. I knew that my foundation had been knocked down and built back up, and that my Self, while cracked and patched in places, was still standing, stronger than before. And I was ready to start building my life upon that solid base.

As I turn the matchbook over in my hand, I remember that day, three years ago, when I emerged from a cocoon of my own making and took flight for the first time, alone—a butterfly on a journey of self-discovery.

—*Cheryl Terpening*

Thanksgiving in Tucson

"**N**o way I'm hiking," eleven-year-old Marisa announced as she rolled out of bed.

"It's okay," Kathy said. "We're getting a late start anyway."

I wanted more than anything to comfort Kathy O'Toole, Marisa's mom and my best friend since kindergarten. And it looked like I wouldn't be able to give her the one thing she had hoped for out loud for this visit.

Of course, just being together for Thanksgiving was great. During the summer, we'd both gone back to New York to visit family, but duties had kept our visits with each other brief. We'd been looking forward to the long Thanksgiving weekend to catch up and to catch our breaths after a difficult year. In that forty-fourth year of our friendship, she'd been hit and hit again with more than her fair share of challenges and heartache. While worrying about her mother's failing health from 2,500 miles away, she had lost her job when her position was eliminated in a corporate merger. Months later, while Kathy was staying in New York to help, her mom died, and her dad's health problems intensified, in part due to his prolonged caregiving and the loss of his partner of more than fifty years. Then, of course, there was September 11, which devastated everyone, especially New Yorkers. Kathy had gone to college, lived, and worked in New York City for years. That was just the big stuff she'd been carrying around inside. Then there was all the "little" stuff she was dealing with, like recovering from an adverse reaction to the drug she'd taken for the infection from a root canal, or the one job interview she'd had since being downsized that didn't go well.

I wanted to help make her feel better, but I was just barely climbing out of my own hole. That I should be in a slump when she was in one was no big surprise. Our lives have always mirrored each other's in strange ways. It is not just that we were in the same Brownie troop, had PTA parents who sewed and baked together, graduated with the same degree from similar small colleges, both married Italian-Americans, had our sons within months of each other, and moved to the Southwest within a year of each other. Though those facts undeniably made for common ground, the connection between us is tighter and deeper than that. Since that first day of kindergarten, when we left our moms standing at the door, if something bad happens to Kathy—though I'm not looking for it, mind you—I'm never surprised if my life hits the fan, too. And if I'm on an upswing, I let her know right away so she can keep her eye out for good luck coming her way. That year had been no exception, though my career snafu and my parents' health issues weren't nearly as serious as hers. But I lost my Grandma Ree just a month after she lost her mom, and I was trying to comfort Kathy while I was stuck smack-dab in the middle of my own grief.

Kathy and Marisa had made the six-hour drive from Southern California to our Tucson home for Thanksgiving. We knew that hanging out together would be good for both of us. I suggested cooking something special in honor of the women we'd lost. She obliged by bringing dough for her mom's famous gingerbread cookies. I made fresh cranberry relish for Grandma Ree. We spent Thanksgiving morning rolling, cutting, chopping, whipping, decorating—all the women things that Betty and Ree had a hand in teaching us and that we now had an opportunity to share with Marisa. As we prepared the feast, Kathy and I talked the way only best friends since kindergarten can talk. We relived experiences that no one else in our lives shared in the same way, and we made new memories that would always be special to just the two of us. She brought out the funny in me, and sometimes I'd start a sentence and she'd nod her head slightly and finish it for me. "I'm not sure why I even bother talking!" I said over the potato peeling.

Thanksgiving was perfect. The meal we prepared tasted delicious. The conversation entertained. Laughter danced around the table. Then it was Friday, the day we'd planned to fulfill Kathy's hope for the weekend. She'd told me a few weeks earlier about the rounded depressions in a large slab of rock she'd seen at the Mission Trails Regional Park near her home in San Diego. At those ancient grinding stones, she had felt connected to the women who'd made them, leaving evidence of their work, preparing grain to nurture their families. Her imagined echoes of their shared conversations touched her heartstrings. She asked if there were any grinding stones in Tucson that we might see. The only spot where Native American grinding stones had been found that I knew about would require two miles of steady climbing into Pima Canyon to get there, and we had a reluctant hiker on our hands.

Tween Marisa was clear: "I'm not hiking four miles round-trip."

I went over other choices. Kathy and Marisa decided on Sabino, where we could take a tram up to the top of the canyon and walk back down. We packed lunch and took off. It was a delightful day, windy but warm. We coaxed Marisa into walking more and riding less on the way back. We enjoyed the sun, the view of the steep cliffs with saguaro cactus sentinels, and the desert's royal blue sky. Knowing early people had lived here, I kept my eyes open, just in case. We found a perfect bathtub shape in a huge rock, scooped out by years of summer monsoons in the now almost-dry riverbed. It wasn't a grinding hole, but it was the closest to one we'd found before leaving the canyon.

As we were stopped at the first traffic light on our way back into town, I pointed up the mountain and said, "I did a two-week program at a school up that road last year."

Kathy turned to look in that direction. "Check out those houses on the mountain!" she said.

Without hesitation, I put on my blinker and turned onto the road. We drove through the grounds of Ventana Canyon Resort to get a closer look at the houses being built on the surrounding cliffs. On the way out, I noticed a sign for trailhead parking.

"Wanna check it out?" I asked. Kathy nodded.

We parked right next to the trail. Marisa preferred to wait in the car rather than join her mother and me for a twenty-minute hike up the trail. We got into a quick pace, hoping to get in as much ground as we could in our mini-hike. Even though we were bushed from our Sabino excursion, it felt good, and the conversation was more candid with just the two of us. As I checked my watch to see how close we were to our ten-minute turnaround time, we both stopped dead in our tracks. In a boulder in the middle of the trail were two grinding holes. Without saying a word, we each bent down and touched the depressions that connected us across time to the women who'd made and used them. Their voices seemed to whisper through the mesquite branches. When we stood up, we high-fived, then turned and started back.

As we approached the last bend in the trail before the parking lot, a female Harris hawk swooped down onto a branch not fifty feet from us. Two young women came up and watched with us. Then an elderly woman and her husband joined us. Three generations of women enjoyed the hawk. Once she'd gotten us all together, talking and admiring her, she flew off. At the trailhead, we parted ways with the other hikers. Kathy and I returned to Marisa, who seemed almost surprised to see us back so soon.

We had found Kathy's grinding holes and, with them, another connection between us and between women who had prepared feasts of thanks before us. We had cooked the honoring foods and passed on to Marisa the tradition of women working together to create a meal. And that Thanksgiving in Tucson, we were there for each other in a way no one else ever could be—as best friends since kindergarten.

—Marge Pellegrino

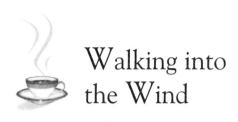

Walking into the Wind

The wind howled, whipping the rain against the den windows. On that angry winter afternoon, darkness began chasing the last rays of daylight shortly after 3:00.

Eden, my four-year-old, had been watching *Sesame Street* with me when she suddenly left my side. She padded to the front hall and for the next several minutes struggled to pull on her boots. I waited for her to ask for my help, but she didn't. Mission accomplished, she yanked her red jacket off the hook.

"Are you going someplace?" I stifled a laugh. Surely, she would soon head for her playhouse in the basement. I would be invited to tea, served through the curtained window of her miniature kitchen.

"To Danielle's." Although tiny for her age, Eden spoke with the assuredness of my forty-year-old boss.

My jaw clamped shut. I refrained from motioning

toward the windows or saying that the storm might suck her all the way to Oz. Her dressing for the weather demonstrated a degree of mature judgment I wasn't about to squelch.

She retrieved her Minnie Mouse umbrella. Her arms, too bulky in the coat, could barely come together to hold the handle. Her sweater must have bunched up at her elbows. I resisted the urge to straighten, watched in silence.

"I'll drive you," I finally said. In good weather, the five hundred yards to Danielle's was an easy walk with no streets to cross.

"I'm not a baby." She opened the door and peeked out.

I could have used the vocabulary of menace— dark, dangerous. Or I could have reminded her that her sister would return from dance class soon, and we would bake cookies.

"How about a kiss?" I said instead.

She beamed at me, her right dimple deepening. Her wet lips left a warm circle on my cheek. Her arms, confined by the jacket, lay for a brief moment against my chest. Then she pushed open the screen door and stepped out.

I dashed to the phone. "Eden's on her way to you," I sputtered to Danielle's mother and hung up. I threw on my coat, drew out an umbrella, and raced into the rain in my rubber-bottomed slippers.

I stayed fifteen feet behind my baby. She struggled with her umbrella against the wind, plodding on, never looking back. In the glow of the streetlight, rain pelted her umbrella and cascaded onto her foot-long back.

This was a rite of passage that I had had no clue was coming. The baby who had learned to walk not long ago already belonged to herself, was already walking away from me into the dark, unafraid. In the storm of the night, my child was lost to me. In her stead appeared the woman who would one day travel the globe.

The rectangular light of an opened door indicated that Danielle's mother waited. Eden was ushered in, never knowing about the salty tears in my mouth.

Before spring, my nine-year-old daughter, Tomm, announced that she was ready for sleep-away camp. Her erstwhile passion for all stray animals—from caterpillars to rabbits—suddenly a childhood fad, she now wanted to attend a drama camp.

"Which of your friends is planning to go?" I asked.

She fingered my earlobe, checking my earrings. "No one."

This was the kid to whom I had relegated emptying the dishwasher when she was only two and a half. And she had never broken a plate. Why was I surprised at her confidence?

In the following weeks as we sat through camp presentations, I stifled my desire to pin my beautiful child to velvet, like a rare and precious butterfly.

"Mommy," she said one night when I tucked her in and settled down to tell her the bedtime stories that were ours alone. She brought her almond-shaped eyes as close as our noses allowed. "When I grow up, I want to be like you, not a PTA mom."

My laughter had the nervous lilt of the guilty career mother. "What's a PTA mom?"

"You have a life."

You are my life, I wanted to say. You and your sister are the center of my universe. But you test me. To pass, I must let you be whoever you want to be rather than the carriers of my hang-ups and fears.

But I didn't say it.

The pink backpack dwarfed her when I put her on the bus to the camp of her choice. Coltish legs poked above her sneakers, and her eyes were dark and grave. Only the huge yellow flower in her hair offset the look of a lost Bambi.

"I don't know anyone," she whispered in my ear, as though the thought had just occurred to her. Her warm breath, with a whiff of her bubble gum–flavored lip-gloss, made me want to take her back home.

"You'll have a friend by the time you get there," I told her.

And she did.

When it was time for Tomm to go to college, she picked the largest institution that had accepted her and several months later took the five-hour train ride for student orientation. I flew in a day later for a parallel parents' meeting. She and I were to meet at the counselor's office.

I sat through the parents' discussion about the anguish of separation, the mourning over being discarded. All around me, befuddled adults agreed that freedom was confusing to their children—and yes, dangerous. As astonishment rose on the horizon of my consciousness, I wondered whether I was missing a secret chromosome. The type of bonding these parents described seemed like a color that eluded the blind me. While I had felt so anchored in my relationship with my Tomm, my parenting must have been flawed all these years for neither of us to feel the angst of separation . . . I hadn't talked with her since she had left the day before. Perhaps she hadn't even arrived. Maybe I shouldn't have let her travel alone or should have at least insisted that she call. And what had made us assume, oh so cavalierly, that the coming months and years would just fall into place?

Suddenly, I wondered whether I should have been a PTA mom. Luckily, I still had a second chance with Eden.

I transferred Eden to a private high school that nourished her insatiable thirst for knowledge and where I could get more involved. But within a couple of years, she charged into adolescence and demanded to return to the public school, where the sandbox for her activities was bigger.

Five years later, on one of her college breaks, Eden took me out for sushi. She had decided to become a movie producer, she said, but only if she could make it big. Did I think it was impractical? It was a flesh-eating industry, she explained, and she'd have to relocate to California. But she had no connections. The easy alternative, she said, would be to make it safely in the New York corporate world. There had been offers for internships.

The dimple of the four-year-old still puckered her right cheek. My baby still walked into the wind, still struggled with her Minnie Mouse umbrella, pelted by rain, unafraid.

My mouth felt cold. My hands around the ceramic tea mug were hot. This was my opportunity—my last—to keep my younger one close and safe.

"You'll make it," I whispered, realizing that my job had always been to get out of the way.

—Talia Carner

Quilting a Legacy

I arrive at my mother's home for our regularly scheduled Monday night family dinner. The smells of chicken and gravy and homemade rolls waft from the kitchen, and all I can think about is pulling off my shoes and resting my feet and my mind before dinner. But my mother is methodically pulling out quilt after quilt from the boxes surrounding her, proudly showing me the handcrafted beauties. She is preparing for the biannual quilt show and sale at the Elmhurst United Methodist Church in Oakland, California. For the past ten years, Mom has overseen the quilting bees at her church. Not only has her group collectively pieced together many of these quilts, but she has also made some of them herself.

She kneels on the soft beige carpet as she unpacks and spreads each quilt on the floor. I get up and examine the quilts, running my fingers over the assorted patterns, admiring the stitching and bounty of fabrics, textures, and fabric patterns. I call out each pattern as I recognize it, trying to remember the names and significance of each pattern.

"Okay, the monkey wrench turns the wagon wheel toward a log cabin, and on to the North Star and Canada," I say. "Hmmm . . . these triangles going in four directions, what do they mean?"

"Those are the flying geese," Mom says, glancing up as she pulls out yet another quilt. "If you put that with other patterns, such as the drunken path and/or crossroads and log cabin patterns, it is a map toward freedom."

It all starts coming back to me, how the different patterns and shapes were used as maps of the Underground Railroad—a coded language for runaway slaves fleeing North to freedom. Slaves would piece together quilts and hang them in windows and on walls, offering direction and comfort to those on the run. What a ray of hope it must have given them, knowing that once they had made the courageous decision to flee slavery, they would be helped along the way by abolitionists. I marvel at this art form that has been handed down from generation to generation, depicting an important chapter in our country's history.

As I admire one of the quilts, the contrasting textures of smooth and raised fabric, I am reminded of a series of presentations that my mother gave a few years earlier during Black History Month. One time I filled in for her. At first, I was nervous. Clutching my notes from the research my mother and I had done, I started off with a little bit of history, facts that few people, including African-Americans, know. My voice cracked slightly as I began to relay the information I'd heard my mother express so easily and effortlessly many times before. But as I continued, the stories of the people who had made the quilts filled me with pride and confidence. As I spoke, the words strengthened me, and I realized that by sharing my ancestors' stories, I was honoring their lives. These courageous African-American ancestors had endured their trials with dignity, and despite innumerable hardships, they had recorded the tale of their remarkable journey, and survival, with art sewn together with needles, thread, and fabric.

After the presentation I was rewarded with appreciative comments and questions. I left feeling content and at peace, realizing that the struggles of those who had made these quilts had not been in vain. Their stories continue to be told in their legacy, their quilts.

My thoughts return to the quilt in my hand, to its vibrant reds, blues, greens, and yellows, sewn by the women of our church, with hands of love and compassion. And so the legacy continues.

As my mother and I share our love of this fine craftsmanship, we point out our favorites among the quilts. Mom holds up a double wedding-ring pattern.

"Flo said one of her coworkers was looking for a wedding gift. This would be nice," she says.

Indeed, the double circles of blue and red swirled into an intricate design would be perfect for the bed of a newlywed couple. We begin to fold the quilts to return them to the boxes, and I notice one quilt still in the bottom of the box. I pull it out.

"What is this?" I ask Mom.

"Oh!" she says, startled. Tears spring to her eyes. "That's Mama's quilt."

She takes it from me and holds it to her chest, lovingly smoothing the fabric with her hands. I look at the quilt more closely. It looks as if a group of grade-school children have pieced it together: an irregular pattern, a slightly crooked seam on the right, a missed stitch above that.

"Grandmother made this?" I say, surprised. My late grandmother was a master quilter. This certainly didn't look like any of the quilts I had seen on her four-poster bed on our summer vacations to Arkansas.

"Mama was well into Alzheimer's when she made this. I brought it home with me last year, and made some alterations and added a few patterns," she said. "I'm still working on it. See, this is what I've done so far."

I look again and see where she has stitched and restitched, going over seams to straighten a crooked angle.

"Look here, in the middle," she says.

I hold it up to the light and see wording stitched into the center. It says:

My mother made many quilts. She was struggling with Alzheimer's and did not know why she could not get things to go right. She had to keep busy. I can hear her say, "Don't show that." I think it is beautiful. I wanted to see it finished. Her last quilt.

"Ooh, this is so nice, Mom," I say, tears now filling my eyes. It suddenly occurs to me that by completing my grandmother's quilt, my mother is paying homage not only to her own mother, but to her ancestors as well.

In Africa, men were the weavers of textiles, but when brought to America as slaves, the women became the seamstresses, as was the European tradition. From her grandmother, a former slave, my grandmother had learned how to make all of the significant patterns: the Grandmother's Garden, which is an array of flowers; the Dresden plate, which is appliquéd with two or four alternating colors; and the North Star, the pattern she'd attempted in her last quilt. How important it must have been for her to do this, to prove that she could continue to quilt at the end of her life.

Cradling my grandmother's quilt, I realize that I hold in my hands a family treasure, a testament to the beauty and strength of my ancestors. It occurs to me that I am only beginning to grasp the power of their story.

Grandmother's last quilt will be displayed at the church on Saturday. But it will not be sold, for it is priceless. Started with the loving hands of one woman, finished by the loving hands of another, it will remain part of the fabric of our family. I, too, will offer my hands to help finish my grandmother's special quilt. And I will continue to piece together the stories of our ancestors with bits of brightly colored cloth arranged in intricate patterns of hope and courage and beauty. And I will pass this quilting legacy of love on to my daughter.

—Dera R. Williams

From Me to We

I must have used the word a thousand times before. Yet, no occasion ever lived up to its meaning until I'd spent six months planning my dream wedding and six hours wearing the white silk dress of a lifetime, and said a foggy and rushed good-bye to every member of our family and every friend we'd ever had. The word is *whirlwind.*

In my case, its definition became crystal clear one Sunday morning at 3:45 (having fallen asleep at 2:15 A.M.) on the way to the airport with wet hair.

For a good part of my thirty-three years, I had wondered how I'd feel the morning after my wedding. Other than a happy kind of fatigue (I now understand how a cat must feel when it purrs), my first distinct emotion didn't come until my eyelids opened wide enough for me to pick out one of the first tiny Caribbean islands as we flew over them.

David had seen them before, but you'd never know it by the way he took my place at the window seat and put me on his lap so we could take in the view together. As he ordered champagne, I realized that my groom had become a present-day Prince Charming with a plain gold band around his finger in place of a crown.

That is exactly the moment I felt the honeymoon—and the transition from "me" to "we"—begin.

While David and I went through the motions of getting our luggage and standing in immigration at the sweltering open airport of Bridgetown, we began to piece together the blur that had been our wedding reception just hours before. "Oh, good, you danced with my niece." "Did you spend any time with Aunt Dee?" "How did our friends end up on stage with the band?"

That is when I noticed the couple in line ahead of us. They, too, wore shiny gold bands on their hands, her hands with a French manicure, like mine. They looked vaguely like us; the only difference was that she had taken the time to dry her hair. They were the first of several newlywed couples we eventually met on our honeymoon who shared our wedding day. Somehow, it made me feel better to meet other brides whose big days had also come and gone in a whirlwind.

But I still couldn't stop thinking about my beautiful gown. The "perfect" dress that had been the shopping challenge a mother and daughter practice years for was lying in a heap on a bed at home.

Once we unpacked, it didn't take long for David and me to realize the difference between a vacation and a honeymoon. A swim doesn't cool you off . . . it heats things up. Dinner isn't the end of a day; it's the dawn of an evening. And meeting new people gives you a chance to get used to referring to each other as "my husband" and "my wife."

David ate with me when he wasn't hungry. In turn, I came close to matching him rum for rum. We slept at the same time, swam at the same time, and shared whatever caught our eye. We saw everything from sea anemones perched beneath a sunken tanker, ogled through goggles, to a sweeping coastline from the top of what we later learned was called "Risk Road," viewed from our rented convertible tin-can-on-wheels. Somewhere along the way, my disbelief over the passing of our wedding day dissolved into excitement for the future of our marriage.

The wedding had started out being about the two of us and ended up being a mass of people we loved but had somehow lost each other in. The honeymoon brought it all back to basics. And there is something about being alone together on foreign soil that reminds you why you fell in love in the first place.

I didn't truly feel like we were family, though, until a full four days after the wedding. There was a glorious sunset that night, but that wasn't it. We dined among palm trees with white twinkle lights for trunks, but that wasn't it. Oddly enough, it was David's smoked fish appetizer that ultimately gave me my first pangs of marriage. He started to feel sick before our main course arrived, and by dessert I knew he was in trouble. We took the first cab we could find and went back to our room. What was happening here? He was the one with food poisoning, yet I hurt.

On the last night of our honeymoon, the resort provided a show of local artists performing the limbo and other phenomena that will stay with us for a good long time. But the most unforgettable moment was when they asked all the honeymooners to stand. I actually thought I could hear what the couples who had been married for years were thinking: "They look so happy. . . . It'll pass."

It was something I had been thinking about as well. How could we keep the magic alive? Though we had been living together for nearly two years, during our honeymoon trip, I fell in love all over again. I didn't want the reality of work and dinners in front of the television to push this feeling too far into the past. I don't expect to feel like a newlywed for-ever. But I would like to keep the image of David's warm brown eyes sparkling with laughter from behind the umbrella of a piña colada nearby when I need it.

The next day while waiting for our shuttle back to the airport, we had yet another meal. When David ordered a salami sandwich and French fries, instead of a flying fish cake and plantain chips, I knew it was, indeed, time to go home.

That was nearly four months ago, and we've had plenty of dinners in front of the television. A few of those meals were spent watching our wedding video. Thanks to the video, the collective stories of our friends and families, and the pictures and journal we kept of the honeymoon, we've been able to fill in the blanks that the whirlwind seemed to obscure.

Somewhere along the way, I've come to understand another word better than ever before: *peace.*

—*Julie Clark Robinson*

To Pearlie, with Love

The holiday season brings with it a barrage of emotions. For some, it is a time of great joy and peace. For others, it represents the most insane time of the year. Sadly, for many, it can be a very lonely time.

Not long ago, I found myself stressed, and not really enjoying the usual holiday preparations. I felt like I needed the Christmas season to be a little different somehow—to hold a deeper meaning than the usual whirl of decorations and gifts and feasts. My husband and I had been blessed with five children, dear family and friends, and work that we enjoyed and that allowed us to live comfortably in our small seacoast community. And at Christmas, we wanted to share life's blessings in a special way.

We wanted to do more than make an anonymous charitable contribution. It seemed too easy and detached to just write a check and buy some toys, wrap them up, and drop them off. I didn't know what exactly we might do, only that I wanted our family to somehow make a difference in someone's life. I wanted a spiritual connection.

"What about adopting a family through the Salvation Army?" my husband suggested.

"We've done that so many times," I told him. Besides, though it was well and good to give things to the needy families participating in the Salvation Army's program, no personal contact was allowed. I wanted to connect with whomever we helped, to know their name, to be able to ask what they needed and wanted, and then to help provide it. I didn't want to read a list of nameless people, knowing nothing about them as individuals, and shop for items someone else instructed me to buy. Convinced that there was someone, somewhere, in whose life we could make a difference in both a physical and a personal way, I continued my search. But all the agencies to which I inquired operated in the same way: just send in the cash or presents, with no person-to-person interaction with those in need.

Poring through a family magazine one evening, looking for craft ideas for my daughter's school party, I read an article about an organization called the Box Project. It told of families being paired with an elderly person or a family in some of the less affluent areas of Mississippi. The aim was to send these folks a care box filled with most anything you pleased once a month. Communication between the parties was encouraged. It was suggested that the boxes sometimes contain items that couldn't be purchased with food stamps, since most families were recipients. The sentence about encouraging communication caught my attention, and I jotted down the phone number and then called to ask for more information.

It seemed like a long wait, but finally I received my packet from the Box Project. Eager to prepare a package for someone in time for Christmas, I filled out my profile, which included an estimate of how much we were willing to spend monthly, and a form agreeing to fulfill this commitment. There was a nominal fee to help cover administrative costs. There was also a cautionary note stating that if requests for items became outlandish or excessive in price, we were to inform the Box Project at once. Therein was the fodder for skepticism. My husband questioned if I was perhaps setting myself up for disappointment.

"What if you pour your heart and soul into this, and find the person on the receiving end to be merely out to get whatever they can for nothing?" he asked.

He had a valid point. My friends shared the same concerns, which, at times, almost bordered on cynicism. They seemed unwilling to believe that most people aren't opportunists. On a leap of faith,

I prepared myself for whatever might come, more determined than ever that our family could make someone's life a little bit better.

The letter came in mid-December, about two weeks before Christmas. I ran into the house and excitedly tore open the overstuffed envelope. The profile I received was of a lady in her late sixties from a rural community south of Jackson, Mississippi. Her name was Pearlie. The information told me about her clothing sizes, gave me a description of where she lived, and made general comments about items that might be of use to her.

I hurriedly sent off a letter of introduction to Pearlie, as suggested in the information packet, and waited for a reply. In just a few days, she answered my letter in the self-addressed and stamped envelope I had sent her. This, too, was a suggestion made by the Box Project. She introduced herself and said she was excited to be a part of the program. She asked for nothing for herself for Christmas, but just a few little things for her five-year-old granddaughter, who was living with her at the time.

Filled with excitement, I enlisted both the generosity and enthusiasm of my daughter's second grade class. In fact, it became their holiday project. Each class member brought in a small item, such as hand lotion, shampoo, bandages, and toothpaste. Some brought items for the little girl, such as crayons, a pad of paper, scissors, hair ribbons, and paints. Together the class wrote holiday greetings to Pearlie and her granddaughter, which we boxed up along with the class donations and sent off to Mississippi.

Meanwhile, at home, our family prepared another box for Pearlie and her granddaughter. We bought some outfits for the little girl and some household items for her grandmother. We included a letter, a Christmas card, and a picture of our family. In the letter, I asked her to please tell me what would be most useful to her, so I'd know what to send the following month.

I was thrilled when Pearlie's next letter arrived not long after. She wrote:

You must have been sent to me by the Lord. Everything was just perfect, and I thank you very much. This is the last month my granddaughter will be living with me. She will go back to live at her mother's in a few days. I will miss her, but am not able to care for her. My daughter is doing better so can have her back in her home. It is nice to send her back with some new things to wear and play with. I love everything you sent. Thank you, thank you, thank you.

Reading along with joy in my heart, I came to the line where she mentioned what she would like me to send the following month:

Could you please send some white cotton underpants, size eight, and some tinfoil?

I was astonished. This lady could have requested anything under the sun. Yet, she had humbly requested cotton underwear and tinfoil.

It has now been more than a year since I began communicating with Pearlie and sending her monthly boxes. Her letters—describing her serious health issues, her move into a subsidized apartment, and her thrill at having access to a washing machine—have been a source of inspiration. Joy for Pearlie has come in the smallest packages. When moving into her apartment, her request was for washcloths. At times, she has asked for things she could give to her daughter. A diabetic, she has delighted in the sugar-free candy I've sent her. A kidney dialysis patient, she has marveled at the little luxuries sent to help her pass the time during her treatments, such as a small cassette recorder and numerous stories on tape. When she mentioned how chilly she sometimes became during dialysis, I sent a hand-knit sweater and lap blanket. She loves receiving sweet-smelling lotions and powders. Most of the things I send are basic items, things many of us take for granted. To Pearlie, they are treasures. Every few months, she still requests some of "that nice tinfoil." I have been happy to oblige.

Last December, I lost my beloved grandmother.

Although she was ready to be with God, it was sad to no longer have her here with me. I mentioned this in a couple of my letters to Pearlie. Shortly after Christmas, I had misplaced Pearlie's biographical information in my post-holiday mess. I wrote to find out when her birthday was.

Her response arrived with the usual outpouring of love and gratitude. She told me she would be honored to have me for a daughter or granddaughter. I felt blessed and honored as well. I turned the letter over to read her last few sentences, and was amazed at what I saw.

"My birthday is February 20," she wrote. So was my grandmother's!

My husband and friends are amazed at the outcome. Initially convinced that I would be met with discouragement and disappointment, they now join me in the sheer delight that comes from being a participant in this wonderful project. It has instilled in our entire family the knowledge that giving is truly better than receiving.

I hope one day to travel to Mississippi and meet Pearlie face to face. In the meantime, our letters and the monthly boxes continue to sustain our growing friendship. Pearlie has given my family something far more valuable than anything contained in the boxes we send. She has given us a little piece of herself, and for that I am truly grateful.

—*Kimberly Ripley*

Duty-Free

Rain splashes the windows as the ferry rocks. We, who have ridden hours trying to see her, peer again through steamed windows and darkness, but the mighty woman with a torch has taken cover for the night. Lady Liberty hides, backlit in heavy mist, leaving us only a blur of wet luminescence.

We have waited years for this: the simple pleasure of riding a whole day—down Seventh Avenue, the ferry to Staten Island and back, the bus up Sixth to the Park, then back down again— together. Two friends, we have come far to reconnect: one across continents and oceans, the other over highways and freeways north, from Maryland. The steady downpour wipes away separation and distractions, syncopates speech, memory, and laughter.

Years ago we worked together. Then we were teachers, serious, learned. Our high heels and dresses made us serious. We were learned to the extent that we had learned a language or two earlier than the students we were teaching, on whom we had at least a decade.

In those days, we had to wait fifty minutes to reconnect, to let the bell mark the end of class five times a day, unleashing adolescents glum from verb conjugation and grammar exercises. The students plowed through the door in search of the day's romantic interest, leaving us to each other and hall duty.

We were young and lucky: to find each other in the same school, with classrooms across the hall. We were lucky to be stuck every year with hall and bus duty—standing together between classes, monitoring drab green-tiled halls, ever-slamming lockers, and slick-as-ice-rink floors, and at day's end, checking the endless line of yellow buses until the last pulled out. We were lucky to have each other during the dirty work of being teachers. Principals roamed the halls, monitoring our monitoring, inspecting suspicious things, whispering into walkie-talkies. But we kept our cover.

We had our real business of talking and laughing. We needed no walkie-talkies. We stayed connected through hall duty sound bites, five minutes on the hour. Like convicts allowed short visits, we laughed and cried and mastered life sharing, while being evaluated on how dutifully we hall-, bathroom-, and bus-dutied. We had been given our charge—to stop students from running, chewing, shoving, kissing, killing, hugging, fighting. We did our duties, looked serious, and kept talking.

These were the years of early adulthood, paying our dues, doing what we had to do. On hall duty, we also raised our children, straightened out our marriages, made decisions, shared fantasies and dreams. In between the precious five-minute breaks, there were thousands of hours spent in square cinderblock rooms: French, room 102; Spanish, room 103—five classes a day, 150 exams a night. It was hard work, but we had hall-, bathroom-, and bus-duty time; each other; and laughter.

Two women in the hall, we wiped chalk dust off our hands and tried to get purple mimeograph ink off our skirts; we taught and we talked. But mainly, in five-minute slices, we carved ourselves out. And we continued sorting out the issues of the day in the parking lot at dusk. Then, packing our own kids and ourselves into a Corvair for spring break and spreading picnics in the summer, we tried to grow up and grow our kids up.

Now there is only the rain, the rocking, and the ferry motor. Slamming lockers and hall huggers are gone; our children are grown. We are beyond lives lived in breaks and sound bites. Today, we have the luxury of twenty-four slow, slippery hours.

I tell you this now: Make early for yourself a

friend who will chew the bones of life with you. Find that one person who will do hall duty, bus duty, child duty, marriage duty, parent duty, work duty beside you. Wipe the dust off your hands together. Expect lives lived on separate continents. Build a fence around memory and laughter. And wait. A time will come—on a bus, a train, or a ferry's deck in the rain—for riding the whole day out past a shrouded woman in the fog, who stands guard over two women lost in unbroken conversation and laughter.

—*Davi Walders*

Well Furnished with Love

We tramped through the forest, enjoying the cooling breezes of the evening. The moon shone between the leaves, guiding us along. My husband led our troop. My mom and dad followed him, muttering about the insanity of not being allowed a flashlight. Our four children filled the middle, and I brought up the rear, relishing the growing darkness. We spoke softly, enjoying the quiet of the woods as much as each other's company.

"If you could be a tree, what kind of tree would you be?" I called ahead.

The older children instantly caught on and began naming trees they'd like to be.

"Well, I've always seen myself as a solid oak," said my father with a wry grin.

"Yeah, Dad, you're definitely a hard wood," I joked.

"What do you think Daddy is?" my eight-year-old asked me.

"He's definitely a red maple, the king of trees," I said.

"I want to be a Christmas tree," piped my three-year-old. "I'm hot, Mommy."

She stopped the procession and peeled off her hooded fleece. I stuffed it into my front kangaroo pocket. Her oldest brother threw me his jacket, too. I tied it around my neck. The middle two boys also unzipped and tossed their jackets to me. I looked more like a child's overstuffed dresser than the sleek willow tree I had envisioned myself to be. With doors hung open, every corner hastily crammed, stuff spilling out of drawers, I was messy but full.

Maybe our characters resemble furniture rather than trees, I thought. I began motherhood as a cradle, waddling through my pregnant days. I rocked and swayed while my baby tumbled and tossed in its cozy cocoon. When I finally laid down to rest, I felt the baby kick off its covers and turn inside me, ready to play.

After their births, I became their crib. I remember holding my second son upright through long sleepless nights. He'd rest his sleepy head across my shoulder, content to feel my heartbeat next to his, as his little brother squirmed and wiggled within my belly. As they grew, I became their footstool, ladder, and sometimes loveseat. A La-Z-Boy can't compare with a mother's arms when sleep plays hide-and-seek with an exhausted child. I tucked droopy heads into the crook of my shoulder and draped dangling legs over my arms, and crooned a quiet, wordless lullaby only we understood.

Come to think of it, I'm the daughter of a workbench. Covered in sawdust and shavings, my father spent hours carving toys, bookshelves, and new furnishings in his little corner in the basement. But he made more than just things on that old workbench. While he sawed, sanded, and carved, I perched across from him and learned the importance of cutting away the dead wood and polishing the good. Now, though, my dad is more of an old-fashioned wardrobe. Deep within him lie treasures and tears I never dreamed existed. He never locks the doors, and though the hinge is rusty and squeaks, he is always happy to invite me in.

My mother has always been more of a big comfy couch—the kind you sink into the moment your bottom touches the cushion. When I came home after a long day at school, I loved to throw myself into her arms. I grew up knowing the wonderful sensation of burying myself in her soft bosom, which always smelled of Noxzema and freshly laundered clothes. Now that I'm an adult and taller than she is, I look to my mother as I would a mirror. She reflects back the real me, not the glorified or faulty version that I sometimes try to pass off as reality. She insists I see myself as I am, without makeup or false hope, with a clear and honest vision.

I'm married to a bookcase. My husband hoards memories and brings them out when we're sitting quietly together. He provides a place for me to set down my worries and a shelf to file away important things that we must not forget. He can be portable or immovable, depending on my needs. He's solid, secured to the wall so that no matter how much I stuff onto that bookcase, it won't fall down. He's my treasure trove of our life together.

And my children . . . they're my hope chest, of course.

—Julia Rosien

Pink Organdy

Esther stood at her closet, trying to decide between the navy suit and the gray wool skirt and cardigan. Esther disliked making choices, but she particularly disliked choosing clothing. Sometimes the effort even gave her a headache.

It wasn't that she had little to wear or that her closet didn't contain a wide variety of fine garments. She just never felt the confidence to choose the right outfit for the occasion.

Today, they would attend a band concert in the park, an outdoor event where the audience sat leisurely on the grass and sipped lemonade through straws. Most likely, the young people would wear jeans, and the middle-aged would wear slacks and sweaters. Esther didn't want to be too dressed down for her age or too dressed up for sitting on a blanket in the park.

She was tempted to call her husband into the bedroom and ask his advice, as she always was throughout their marriage, though she had never given in to that temptation. Once again, she fought the urge. Getting a grip on herself, she pulled out the gray skirt and cardigan, looked at each piece, sighed, laid them on her bed beside the pearls he'd given her for her birthday, and started to change.

Suddenly, a distant memory entered her mind—one that had broken her teenaged heart all those years ago.

He was three years older than she, a popular high school senior; she was a lowly sophomore. They shared no classes together, and their paths never crossed, but she had seen him often from afar. And to her, he was the most magnificent boy she had ever laid eyes on. Tall and slender, he had brown hair with a wave that fell over his forehead and shoulders perfect for leaning on. He wore white canvas shoes, which gave him a devil-may-care appearance that she somehow knew in her heart was not really like him at all.

Through sly detective work, she found out his classes and his homeroom. She also learned that his first name was Alan. But she never approached him, never so much as said hello. Then, at the end of the school year, she heard something from other girls at school that made her heart thump in her chest: He had a summer job bagging groceries at the store where her mother worked as a cashier.

Her mother usually did the grocery shopping at the store before she came home from work, so there was no reason for Esther to go there. But realizing that Alan would probably leave for college at the end of summer inspired Esther to do something she would never have done otherwise. She stopped by the store one Saturday for a pack of gum. Her mother couldn't help but notice Esther's gaping mouth as she stood at the cash register looking out the window to the parking lot. Alan, the muscles in his arms and back straining against his white T-shirt, that devilish strand of hair gleaming in the sun, seemed to float across the parking lot in those white shoes as he helped an elderly woman load her car with shopping bags.

"Esther, are you all right?" her mother asked, grasping her arm, no doubt fearing that her daughter was about to faint. Esther wondered the same thing.

She was so taken with seeing the boy she'd adored from the other end of school hallways and across school lawns that she couldn't speak. Her hands shook, and she felt queasy with fear and embarrassment. She couldn't let him see her. Without a word to her mother, she ran from the store and all the way home, slammed the door behind her, flopped down on the couch, and cried.

"Esther," her mother said when she got home from work and found her daughter in her room, deep in the pages of a novel. "Why don't you ever go out? All you do is sit in this room and read. Other girls belong to clubs and go out on dates and go shopping together. All you do is read."

Esther sulked behind her book. Her mother always tried to get her to join in, but Esther was usually content with her books and record player. Besides, she got out enough to suit herself. She attended high school football games, didn't she? She visited the library every Saturday, didn't she? What more did her mother want?

"I want you to be happy, Esther. I want you to meet a nice boy," her mother said.

Esther put down her book. "I don't want to meet a nice boy, Mama."

"Well, you will meet him. He saw you at the store today and told me he wants to ask you out, to a dance at the university," her mother said.

Esther jumped up. "Mama! I don't want to go to a dance! And I don't have anything to wear!"

"You have a closet full of clothes, Esther."

"But—"

"Yes, I know, you have nothing suitable for a dance. I'll give you the money to go downtown and choose something lovely. You'll have a wonderful time at the dance."

What choice do I have? Esther thought. She'd always done what her mother asked. Well, she'd go, but she wouldn't dance. She would say she didn't know how. She would say she'd hurt her foot.

"Who is the boy?" she asked, dejected.

Her mother smiled. "You'll like him, Esther. He's very nice. He's the new bag boy at the store."

Esther's heart fell to her toes. It couldn't be! She couldn't do it! She wouldn't be able to speak! She'd spend the entire evening shaking!

Esther had no idea what to wear to a dance, especially at the university. She milled around the store, leafed through all the dresses, and finally chose a knee-length, pink organdy dress with a high collar and elbow-length sleeves. Then she realized she had no shoes to wear with it. It was the fad then to buy cloth-topped shoes and have them dyed to match the outfit. Esther went home with pink shoes.

The dance was a disaster. Esther sat in a corner, trying to be pleasant but totally forlorn. The university girls, with upswept hair, long pencil-slim black skirts, and scoop-necked or off-the-shoulder blouses, seemed so much older and more sophisticated than she felt. No one wore pink shoes. Everyone danced except Esther and, she was certain out of sheer kindness, Alan.

While Esther was panicking inside and willing

herself to fade into the nearest wall, Alan seemed to enjoy himself. He talked with her, smiled at her, circled the rim of the dance floor to fetch her soft drinks and snacks, and talked with passersby. But with each look at the dance floor and all those lovely university girls, Esther felt more out of place, more ashamed that she had ruined Alan's evening and his chance to dance with the prettiest of them.

At home that night, she buried her face in her pillow and sobbed. She would never, ever show her face to Alan again. She had made such a fool of herself, wearing pink organdy and pink shoes like a six-year-old in a Sunday school play, sitting in a corner, unable to dance, like the wallflower she was.

Alan called her the next week to ask her out again. No way. Never. She was completely humiliated, and she was certain she had humiliated him as well.

Esther felt a hand on her shoulder.

"Almost ready?"

She turned toward him, straightening her sweater over her skirt. Gray skirt. Gray sweater. Gray hair.

"You look lovely," he said.

"Thank you, but I'm all gray."

"But when you smile at me," he said, stroking her hair, "Your cheeks turn a radiant pink, and your eyes are like a starlit evening sky."

"Do you think I'll pass, then?"

"More than pass, my beautiful Esther."

He took her into his arms, and she felt completely loved and protected in his warm embrace.

"But you know, Esther," he said, "as beautiful as you are now, you'll never look lovelier than you did the night I fell in love with you, in your pink organdy and pink shoes."

She snuggled against Alan's chest and knew she had made the right choice about much more than pink organdy.

—*b.j. lawry*

Monday Morning

"We can play in the RAIN! It will be so FUN! I love the RAIN!"

I wake up to the sound of William singing to himself. There is no real tune except that the last word of each line is slightly higher in pitch and volume. I roll over to squint one eye at the alarm clock: 6:35. I close my eyes, hoping that somehow it's not 6:35, it's not Monday morning, and I don't have to be out the door with William in about an hour.

"And the RAIN! It came DOWN! It's so WET! Go away, RAIN!"

The singing persists. I lie in bed and think about what is to come: We are about to begin the daily tug-of-war, William pulling me toward the world of pretend and me pulling him toward the reality of picking out clothes, eating breakfast, and getting to school and work. I'm already frustrated, because I know how to win this game, and he doesn't even know he's playing.

I drag myself out of bed and stumble up the stairs to William's room. He is lying on his Winnie the Pooh sheets, legs spread-eagled, wearing his Toy Story jammies, which I just then realize are on the edge of too small. When he sees me, he sits up, smiling. His hair is doing its usual crazy morning dance with swirls and eddies all over the crown. I almost never have time to tame this nest and won't today. Instead I kid with his day-care workers that he is doing his Ethan Hawke grunge imitation.

William starts talking as if the night that has just passed was merely a pause in our ongoing conversation.

"Backhoes get dirty."

"Yes, they do, William."

"The wheels get dirty when they drive."

"Okay, sweetie." I am using my patient voice. "Let's leave the backhoes for a minute. I need you to pick out clothes, because we have to get moving this morning. You have to go to school, and Mommy needs to go to work. Your green pants and your stripy turtleneck are clean. Do you want to wear those?"

"But why do the wheels get dirty, Mommy?"

"William." There is now an edge to my voice. "We can talk about the backhoe later. Right now, we need to concentrate on picking clothes. Do you want to wear the stripy shirt?"

"But, Mommy, why do the wheels get dirty?" His voice goes up in pitch.

"William, if you don't answer my question, I will just pick out your clothes for you!"

"But don't pick out my clothes!" He's raised his voice to meet mine. He slowly drags himself over to his dresser, laboriously opens a drawer, and pulls out a short-sleeved shirt. It's December.

"You can wear that if you pick out a sweatshirt," I say, knowing this will cause an argument later. He agrees.

When we get downstairs, it's 6:52, and I'm roughly on schedule. I head to the kitchen and put on the water for tea.

"Mommy, will you play with me?" William is holding a dump truck in one hand and offering me a small Tonka grader.

"Buggy, we really don't have time right now. I would like to, but we're very late."

We're not actually late yet, but this sentence is a reflex in the mornings. "Now, what do you want for breakfast? You can have cereal, a bagel, or eggs and toast." I want to bite my tongue as I say "eggs and toast." It's his favorite, but he will want to help.

Sure enough, he cries, "Eggs and toast!"

After I break three eggs into the bowl, William stands ready with the eggbeater. I resign myself to his "help," but regret this as I watch the countertop get splattered with a sticky, yellow slick. "Watch what you're doing, William. Please keep the eggs in the bowl!"

My sharp tone of voice makes him look up at me. "I'm sorry, William, but we're late!"

At last, William is seated. He's piled all of his eggs on top of his jellied toast and is driving this concoction around his plate, making the sound of a fire engine.

By 7:37, I've showered and dressed while William watches *Sesame Street.* Ideally, we'd be backing out of the garage in three minutes, but that looks doubtful. We've got more dressing to do. When I bring William his boots, he greets me with, "Mommy! Look what I can do!" He is sitting astride one of the arms of the easy chair as if riding a horse. I keep myself from saying, "We're late!" and manage a halfhearted, "Great!" as I start pushing the hiking boots onto his floppy feet.

"These are my construction boots, right, Mommy?" He says "construction" with determination and seriousness, elongating the middle syllable, eyes squinting with effort. It's not that he's struggling with the word; it's just that construction is serious business for William. Then we have to confront the sweatshirt.

"William, you need to put on your sweatshirt."

"But, I'm not cold," he insists. It's now 7:42.

"William, you may not be cold now, but it will be cold in the car. Put your sweatshirt on. Now."

"But . . . I've got a good idea!" He changes tactics. "I could put it on once I'm in the car!"

"Not while you're buckled in your car seat. Put it on here!" My voice is getting frantic.

"But Heather and Rachel say—" This is his final strategy: appeal to the wisdom of his teachers.

"William!" I explode. "We are not going to do this today. We are not. I am going to put on your sweatshirt for you. We are really late, and you must wear your sweatshirt. If this makes you cry, I'm sorry."

It does. And I am.

As William climbs into the backseat, his eyelashes are still wet, but the tears have subsided to a slight shiver when he inhales. I maneuver into the driver's seat. The dashboard clock says 7:47 as I back out of the garage and turn on the radio to catch the news. I half listen to an interview with a military expert about the technology of the Gulf War.

As I stop for the red light at the entrance to our neighborhood, William is pushing one of his trucks around his lap, making quiet engine noises. The interviewer asks the expert about "smart bombs."

". . . and they can go down a chimney and into someone's living room," the voice explains.

"Mommy! Mommy!" William is breathless. I glance in the rearview mirror. His eyes are wide and shining, his lips slightly parted. In a reverent tone, he breathes, "They're talking about Santa Claus!"

As the light turns green and we merge into the Monday-morning traffic, William asks, "Mommy, why are you crying?"

"I'm okay, Buggy," I say as I look in my rearview mirror at my child's shining face. It suddenly doesn't matter that we are late again, that our countertops are constantly sticky with egg, that William will never leave the house with all of his hair going in the right direction. William's innocent confidence that it is only Santa Claus who comes down chimneys forces me to see the world through his eyes. The tension, the hurry, the irritation of the morning fades in the face of my son's innocent beauty. William is four years old, and he believes in Santa Claus.

—Ellen Jensen Abbott

NA3yk

 # Must Be Wednesday

I always knew it, of course. My friends are very, very important.

I always thought that was a good thing, or if not good, just part of who I am. But when my husband said, "Your friends are too important," it became different—an accusation, a reason for my children's pain. I promised I would change. I told him the calls to Mary would stop; my excitement over trips to visit Doris would end. I gave him a laundry list of how my behavior could be modified, but it was all in vain.

"You cannot change you," he said, and then he left.

Of course, he had always been a master in effective diversionary tactics—picking something that would provoke guilt, something inherently unchangeable, and, most important, something not about him. For a while, it worked—until I found out about *his* very important friend, who, coincidentally, became his wife not long after the divorce.

When that happened, my friends showed up, one by one. Listening, organizing, cajoling, crying, laughing, they helped me to reclaim who I'd been and to move toward what I could be. Sometimes I looked at their devotion with so much wonder that it took me a while to see the truth behind it.

This is what women do. We show up.

And we never give up on good friendships. Never. It is just part of being female, and if it isn't the best part, it is a pretty wonderful one. As we go through the different stages of our lives, each with its distinctive tone and circumstances, our friendships have a unique ability to provide what is needed to help us survive and, ultimately, to thrive.

Although I've known this all along, I have grown increasingly more aware and drawn to the miracle of being, and having, girlfriends. This recognition perked up my ears and made me pay attention. It finally took me to the house of Joyce Ebner, who lives five miles from me.

I did not know Joyce. She was a friend of some of my friends. It is through these mutual friends that I heard about Joyce and arranged to interview her.

"If I can touch what is going on with Joyce," I thought, "I can touch magic."

I went to the interview expecting to be depressed. I left feeling overwhelmed with beauty.

Over the years, Joyce Ebner had accumulated many friends, and these friendships evolved. When discussions about colic ended, they turned into conversations about PTA meetings. When PTA meetings and after-proms were history, they talked about the high school basketball team (one of Joyce's many interests), politics, and the world. In these respects, Joyce and her friends are not unlike any other group of good women friends anywhere.

The markers of her life are impressive and would be intimidating if they were not mixed with the added gifts of grace and humility. She earned a Ph.D. in microbiology by the age of twenty-six. With her devoted husband of over thirty years, she has raised six children, two of them doctors. A star in her investment club, she is an expert in finance. But the most powerful thing about Joyce—the essence running through her life—is her faith. It permeates the air around her and sets the tone for everything else.

Last August, Joyce started experiencing an unusual weakness in her legs. At first, the doctors were uncertain of the diagnosis. In October, she was diagnosed with amyotrophic lateral sclerosis (ALS, or Lou Gehrig's disease). ALS is an incurable autoimmune disorder that gradually destroys the nerves that control the muscles and, eventually, the organs. Weakness leads to eventual paralysis, but while ALS systematically destroys the body, it leaves the mind untouched.

As the disease progressed, a wheelchair became necessary. Then, a ventilator was added. And that is when the world of Joyce and her friends underwent another transformation. It became clear that although Joyce had a dedicated and loving family and was an independent individual, she needed outside help for some of the details of life. Jan Coleman, one of her friends, was inundated with calls from other friends who wanted to do something. So, she approached the family.

"Everyone wants to help," she said. "Let me organize it."

And she did. About eighty women currently work together in committees to help Joyce. There is the food committee, organized by Joyce's friend Marty, which consists of about fifty women who supply meals to the family three to four times a week. There is a spiritual committee of people from Joyce's church, which brings her communion and prays with her at the start of the day.

There is a morning "caregiver" group, as they call themselves. But that seems too clinical for what they are to Joyce and what they do for her. These are Joyce's best friends: Sally, Jan, Joann, Charlcie, and Judy. They each have a day. Their days never change. So you can tell which day of the week it is by the car in Joyce's driveway.

Why do they do it?

"Joyce would have been the first to do this for

us," her friends said.

Joyce's best friends help her start her day five days a week. They come at around 8:00 in the morning and leave at 1:30, so as to give the family both needed assistance and private time. They bathe Joyce and do her hair. They help with her physical therapy. There is a substitute list of people they can call if something comes up, but that rarely happens, as they are very protective of their mornings.

The friendships that began with PTA meetings now have a more intimate tone. The boundaries have been washed away; the communication is different. Nothing is taken for granted; no time goes to waste; no important words are left unsaid.

But some things remain the same. Every morning at 11:30, Joyce sits down with one of her friends, who feeds her some coffee. Then, if the friend happens to be distracted with cleaning up the kitchen, Joyce gives her a fierce look, and the friend knows it is time to sit down and talk. And so, the friend talks—about the most recent high school basketball game, or politics, or what's going on in the world.

Sometimes, everything changes, and yet nothing changes. The sun comes up. A good cup of coffee is brewed. A friendship is shared.

Today, an Audi station wagon sits in Joyce's driveway. It must be Wednesday.

—*Sue Vitou*

Look in the Mirror, Darling

Aunt Sadie slept on a satin pillow designed to keep her hair in place. It looked like an ordinary pillow to me. But Aunt Sadie told me that if I'd look closely, I could see it was a magical pillow, with bumps and curves scientifically proven by researchers at MIT to keep hair looking like you had left the beauty salon only minutes before. That was Aunt Sadie's story, and she stuck by it. That pillow was one of her most prized possessions, and she swore by it.

"Nine dollars and ninety-five cents for a pillow that keeps me attractive, makes the men look. Who could ask for more?" Aunt Sadie said.

Who was I to argue with researchers from MIT? Who was I to argue with my Aunt Sadie? Who was I to doubt that magic existed, even in the form of a pillow?

But why Aunt Sadie wanted her hair to remain locked for a week in a stiff, sticky, fluffed-up gray sculpture, lacquered with so much hair spray a tornado wouldn't have ruffled a single hair, was beyond me.

"Aunt Sadie," I'd say. "This is the nineties. Get with it. Hair should look natural."

Aunt Sadie wasn't interested. She was eighty years old; asking her to try something new was futile. Besides, she liked how she looked, and she adored the ritual of having her hair embalmed every Friday afternoon at three o'clock. It gave her *naches* (pleasure).

It was a generational thing. Sadie's sister, my aunt Rose, also went to great lengths to make sure her do stayed in place. Aunt Rose's special method of hair control was to wrap her head in toilet paper at night. It reminded me of the way cotton candy is rolled at the circus: Round and round the white sugary layers of candy spin, until a cone is formed. Round and round Rose twirled the toilet paper, until her head was covered with a white turban to keep her cotton-candy-stiff hair in place.

It seemed to me that my aunts wanted their hair to look like neatly trimmed bales of hay awaiting a portrait by Monet, the gray bundles of beauty in twilight he'd never painted. But though fashions changed from week to week and technology brought dramatic changes to our daily lives, Rose and Sadie's beauty rituals did not change with the passing of time. And while the golden years brought changes to my aunts' bodies—making it difficult for them to open jars and walking an aerobic challenge—their stiff-as-a-board-hair rituals never changed. It was as if they were caught in a time warp. And they continued their campaign to instill in me the importance of feminine rituals.

I was a hard nut to crack. Refusing their methods of hair control, I continued to let my hair hang free, flinging it wildly like a horse's mane before their disbelieving eyes.

"No good will come from your behavior," they warned.

Then, they changed tactics. With hope in their eyes, they introduced me to another feminine ritual: jewelry wearing. This will tame her, they thought.

"There is always room for jewelry, just like there is always room for Jell-O," Aunt Sadie said. We were a family of dessert eaters; maybe that would work.

And so my aunts presented me with lemon Jell-O molds garnished with pearls and pins, rhinestones, and opals. When I still refused, they turned up the heat.

"Where's the jewelry?" they would chant whenever I came to visit.

"I don't wear any, I don't wear any," I'd chant back.

That I never wore jewelry and refused their repeated coercions to wear the jewelry they gave me became a source of great pain for my aunts.

"Everyone has to wear jewelry," they lamented. "It's un-American not to wear jewelry."

"I suppose J. Edgar Hoover will be at my door next week to arrest me," I replied.

"Don't be smart with us, young lady," said my Aunt Sadie. "He's much too busy to visit you." (Didn't I tell you they lived in a time warp?)

My aunts were unwavering in their resolution to win me over to their feminine ways. They dangled gold and silver trinkets before me. They insisted I take expensive treasures home and give jewelry a chance. They were certain I'd come around to their view of jewelry as a necessity in the modern world. They argued that all real women wear jewelry.

Aunt Sadie said, "What's wrong with you?"

Aunt Rose said, "It won't kill you to wear a bracelet. Be a person already. Wear some jewelry."

"A little rouge wouldn't hurt either," added Aunt Sadie.

"No jewelry!" I said, to deaf ears.

The more insistent they became, the more resistant I became—until I was as crazy as they were and refused to wear anything that glittered, shook, clanged, or sparkled.

It was more than they could bear. They wept. And though I stubbornly held strong, I began to wonder, was my victory worth their tears?

At Aunt Rose's eighty-seventh birthday party, my aunts started in again with their jewelry routine, like two characters on an old radio show. I remembered how, when I was young, my mother had told me to choose my battles wisely. And I remembered how they had wept. I knew jewelry was not worth the fight anymore, and I agreed to take home an opal ring and a silver bracelet. My aunts proudly removed their baubles and gave them to me in a historic moment, my initiation into the society of womanhood. It was such a small thing to do to make two elderly ladies I loved happy.

Today, I buy costume jewelry any chance I get. I have become a collector of the gaudy and inexpensive. Does this make me feel more like a woman? I hate to admit it, but yes, it does, a little. But mostly I do it to honor Aunt Rose and Aunt Sadie.

I can see them now in the next world, coaxing the angels, "You want to feel like a real person? Do something with your hair, already. Try a spot of rouge, right here. Wear a little jewelry. You'll feel so much better, darling."

—*Elizabeth P. Glixman*

Boundless Gifts

"Y̶ou want to be a mom, Jules, because you have such a good one."

The moment a friend made this observation, the truth in it suddenly became clear to me. My mother had taught me so much about maternal love that I couldn't wait for my turn to show what a good student I was. It was simply a matter of wanting to share.

I long to create an environment so safe and warm that my children are limited only by their imagination. Now that my sisters and I are grown women, we marvel at the games we fabricated as children. A stepladder wasn't something for Dad to paint with; it was the lifeguard station we used to turn our front yard into a swimming pool. During the summer of 1972, our driveway wasn't for cars, it was our personal quest to color every stone in the path with our giant crayon box.

Because of my mother's love, I always felt I was the prettiest, smartest, and most special girl in my class. Imagine my surprise to look back at my school photos and see otherwise. Nevertheless, my mom's positive reinforcement worked. As a result, I entered the adult world equipped with the confidence that I could handle it. And even when, over the years, it has turned out that I could not, my mom's warm voice still gives me the reassurance I need from time to time.

My two sisters began their turn at motherhood years before I did. My older sister hasn't missed a softball, basketball, or football game—powder puff or otherwise—in eighteen years. My younger sister's daughter has taken my place as the prettiest, smartest, and most special girl in the class. As a result, five lucky young people will one day make good parents to other lucky young people.

I wasn't entirely aware of it at the time, but looking back, I think I fell in love with my husband, David, in part because I knew he would make a great father. Every time his eagle eye spots a flea on our Dalmatian and he carefully launches a search-and-destroy mission against the intruder, I feel happy for our unborn children. Every time he stares at some-thing as simple as a fence, I know he's not merely looking at a fence, he is analyzing the engineering of the fence. And I feel happy for our unborn children.

I felt happy for our unborn children at Easter, when David's dad, the patient grandfather-in-waiting, had me, David, and David's thirty-five-year-old sister running around the yard in our jammies, looking for colored plastic eggs with candy and money inside.

David and I share the same thrill at the onset of thunderstorms and blizzards. We enjoy trick-or-treat night more than any other adult on our block. There's yet to be a task I can't make a game out of, and David's been building a tree house in his mind since he outgrew his own. All of this makes me feel happy for our unborn children.

I can't think of a purer image of joy than a freshly bathed infant nestling against my neck. But my vision of motherhood extends so much farther: past building blocks and arithmetic; past snow forts and lemonade stands; past the first date and even the last night under our roof before setting out into the world.

After graduating college, I thought I'd have plenty of opportunities to make my mark on the world. But with an advertising career of more than ten years under my belt, I doubt that any of my work will do more for the general public than perhaps help them to cope with the heartbreak of psoriasis. Now that I'm well into adulthood, I believe that the best gift I can give my little corner of the world is an emotionally strong, kind human being—or two. Maybe the best legacy I have to pass on is a love of loving.

With the pregnancy we're now planning, I'm feeling something so familiar and yet so distant—like a giddy visit from someone I knew long ago. Even with the cloak of reality that automatically travels with anyone in their mid-thirties, I actually feel my heart race with anticipation in a way it hasn't since I was that prettiest, smartest, most special girl, waking up on Christmas morning to a roomful of surprises.

Only this time, the gift will last for the rest of my lifetime . . . and then some.

—*Julie Clark Robinson*

Traveling Companion

I ngrid and I stroll the plaza of Rue Prince Arthur, pausing now and again to look over handmade jewelry, to peek in windows of artsy clothing boutiques, to admire elegant displays of pottery. Six blocks of the avenue are closed to traffic, and artisans, musicians, tourists, and residents alike come together in a colorful street-fair atmosphere.

We stop to watch an artist at work on a pastel portrait of a happy young couple. The young man's face has already been sketched in, but the artist is now bringing the young woman to life. He selects just the right shade of aquamarine to capture her shining eyes and a warm coral that gives fullness to her adoring smile.

Ingrid and I have "happy couple" pictures at home, taken back when our spouses were our "squeezes." On a late summer afternoon, the four of us had taken a cruise on their old boat. My husband, then boyfriend, encircles me with his arms as I lean back into his shoulder, and our auburn hair shines fiery against the teal backdrop of Lake Ontario. Today we do not sit quite as close. Stress eating into our already stormy marriage has contributed to an increased distance between us. His hair is no longer the same color as mine; he is now completely gray, due in part to genetics and in part to illness.

In Ingrid's couple picture, her boyfriend-now-husband looks all of fifteen, which he did for many years. Today, at forty-four, he finally looks to be in his thirties, but the telltale lines around his eyes reflect the worry over his wife's deep disappointment from infertility. Ingrid's young and wiry body has changed and softened, too, for countless reasons. Medication and stress have had their role, but mostly the casualty of many miscarriages, followed by the cycles of grief for children who never came.

The applause from up ahead beckons, and we join the circle surrounding a young man on a unicycle juggling torches. We watch, smiles flickering across our faces. In one final graceful move, he tumbles forward from his perch, bows deeply, and rolls his battered top hat down the length of his arm. We search our pockets for a handful of coins to show our appreciation.

Farther on, the enticing scent of lamb infused with lemon, oregano, and garlic fills the night air. We take a table on the plaza outside a Greek restaurant. Ingrid and I have chosen a wonderful Cabernet, and the waiter quickly arrives to uncork our selection.

I know that Ingrid shouldn't be drinking. It's probably not the best idea with her medication. But we're on vacation, for heaven's sake, and to her mind, life is a series of choices, none of them absolute.

"I don't believe that, in the long run, perfect attendance gets you anywhere," she says.

We savor the first sips as we study our menus. The fare is Greek, but the menu is printed in French, and I translate for her. "*Agneau;* that's lamb. *Poisson* is fish. *Avec des épinards,* that means with spinach."

We've translated for each other frequently in our travels, Ingrid relying on her family's native German and I on my fractured high-school French. Along the way we learned a few phrases in other languages, among the most important: "A cup of coffee, please," and "How much is this?" I'd never before had to translate the words for marriage or miscarriage.

It happened while we were talking with some young French-Canadian travelers. They wondered what a couple of middle-aged women were doing at the Montreal youth hostel. I explained that, yes, we're both married, but our husbands don't appreciate our style of travel. They naturally inquired about children: "*Avez-vous les enfants?*"

I glanced furtively at Ingrid. Her lips straightened,

and she nodded slightly. My husband's illness and my hormonal storms have kept us from having children, and Ingrid and her husband have been unsuccessful as well. I haltingly tried to explain, trying the literal translation. *"Elle a perdu les enfants." Perdu*—to lose.

They looked at each other quizzically: *Perdu?* "Ah," said one, *"Tombe! Les enfants tombe!"*

"Tombe," I repeated to Ingrid—to fall. Somehow the translation didn't work for us. Falling doesn't seem to capture the emptiness or the grief in the same way that losing does.

We begin with an appetizer plate; for our tastes and limited budgets, it is a magnificent bargain at $5.95 Canadian. It enables us to choose the lamb as our main course, and to sample a bit of this and a taste of that. Soon, we are savoring *dolmades* (grape leaves), *spanikopita* (spinach in filo pastry), *tara-masalata* (a spread of caviar, feta cheese, and kalamata olives)—stirring memories of our time in Greece, a grand finale to the summer we'd spent traveling together fifteen years earlier.

"I like eating with people who say 'mmmmm,'" says Ingrid. We say "mmmm" a lot this weekend.

We both agree that we miss this kind of travel; it's been far too long since 1980 when we spent the summer backpacking across Europe together, touring eleven countries with our Eurail passes. Our trip was a meandering, serendipitous vagabond experience. We took trains with one destination in mind, but if a station looked interesting or a fellow traveler recommended a certain town or museum or restaurant, we'd take a little detour.

So it was that we stumbled into some of the most wonderful moments of our trip. An impromptu stop in St. Wolfgang, a tiny village on an Austrian alpine lake, found us arriving in the midst of a 500th-anniversary heritage festival. We spent the evening among costumed villagers in lederhosen and dirndl skirts, enjoying the echoing *oompahs* of brass bands in the village square. In Greece, we took a spontaneous daylong moped ride around the island of Corfu. A late morning dip in the Ionian Sea was followed by a lunch of stuffed tomatoes, Greek salad, and wine at a sun-drenched table overlooking the tiny circular harbor of Kouloura. We sat leisurely with eyes half-closed as the salt dried to a silky powder on our sun-tanned skin. Then there was the wonderful night we decided to take the "Orient Express" out of Paris, and spent the evening drinking strong coffee in a smoky jazz club in the Latin Quarter until departure time at one minute past midnight.

The next morning begins the way we've begun each morning in Montreal—with a first round of latté in our room. One of us tucks her nightshirt into a pair of jeans, slips on a pair of sandals, and dashes braless and unbrushed into the streets to a nearby café or cappuccino cart, returning with our treasure, our habit, our sustenance, our luxury. We sip as we dress, breathing in the spicy, warm aroma of the freshly roasted brew.

Once clothed and ready, we search out a cozy café where we take our formal breakfast. We order a second round of latte accompanied by warm, buttery almond-filled croissants. Over the third cup and a second pastry, we spread out our books and maps and plan the day.

Three cups of coffee! Ingrid's husband would be furious. As with the wine, her medication makes her sensitive to caffeine. He doesn't like it when she drinks too much; she gets a little "overstimulated" and chatters at a dizzying rate. But I'm fine with that. Chatter and laughter are precisely what we seek this weekend.

Then we begin our meandering exploration of the narrow cobbled streets of Vieux Montreal, the old city, admiring the buildings capped with ornate tile roofs and adorned with wrought-iron trim. Worn stone steps lead into shops, and the interiors are usually exposed brick with tin ceilings or exposed wooden beams. We wander into and out of shops, admiring often but buying seldom. As always, money is a factor.

In our earlier European summer, we carefully counted our Deutsche marks and drachmas, walking an extra block or two just to get a slightly better exchange rate. We survived on crusty French bread fresh from the *boulangerie* and rich blue cheese from the *fromagerie,* or soft pitas with feta washed down with red peasant wine plucked from a deep tray of cool water on a table outside a local farmer's home. You'd get 50 drachmas back when you returned the empty bottle to be refilled and resold.

Today money is still a factor, and we search the banks for the best Canadian exchange rate. Ingrid is saving her money for the day when they hope the call will come that a child is waiting for them to love. I'm mindful of the stacks of credit card bills that we accumulated by necessity when I found myself out of work for the second time in as many years. It was a joint decision that permitted me to forgo working and return to school full time, finishing my degree twelve years after I started. But it's a decision that we are still paying for.

We wander into one boutique scented with rose-petal potpourri. The shelves are full of handmade writing papers, decorative journals, cards, wrapping paper by the sheet, hand-milled soaps tied with raffia, bottles of bath oils, and wicker baskets overflowing with natural sponges. These items speak to the deepest parts of both of us. I drift dreamily from shelf to shelf, caressing the textures of the papers, imagining the things I would capture in the journal pages, the thoughts I would send to friends on the beautiful greeting cards.

Ingrid loses herself in the scented soaps. She lives in a quaint little tumbledown cottage on the lake. Its floors are uneven, the cabinets are rustic, and the windows groan against the winter storms. Her one luxury is the newly remodeled bathroom with a deep Jacuzzi tub. A custom-arched window next to the tub looks out onto the lake.

We each select one inexpensive item. I choose a card with a watercolor café scene, which I'll send to Ingrid at a later date, perhaps when she is sad again, to remind her of our time in Montreal. Ingrid chooses an elegant bottle of bath oil infused with herbs and flowers and sealed with a cork dipped in wax and tied with a ribbon. This will sit next to her new tub, and matches the colors of the flowers on the hand-painted tile trim.

The last night in Montreal we choose another Greek restaurant, this one specializing in seafood. We do it up big tonight. Again an appetizer plate, but this time followed by *homard* (lobster) served with a Greek salad and crispy seasoned potato wedges. Ingrid tosses it all to the wind and decides that tonight we will have wine and coffee both! No perfect attendance for her!

The waiter is amused at the size and variety of our order. He laughs and returns often to joke with us. "You know," he says, "not many women order, or eat, with such passion. This is good. You are not afraid to enjoy."

When he returns to offer dessert, he begins to explain the choices. "The baklava . . . and," he says, "a custard with a pastry crust—"

"Yes!" we cry in unison. "*Galactoboureko!*"

"Of course!" he says. "You know this. I will bring you two."

And so they are on the house for us. We dip into the delicate custard sprinkled with orange peel and laced with orange-nutmeg syrup. We follow it with strong coffee that will keep us chattering and laughing until the early morning hours. That is what we are here for, after all.

Over the years, Ingrid and I have been served some unpleasant surprises—misfortunes and tragedies that threaten to nibble away at our confidence, our resources, our faith, and our strength. But my traveling companion and I have gone out into the world with hearty appetites, and we eat life abundantly!

—*Karen Deyle*

 No Longer Strangers

A few years ago, the strain between us was still painfully obvious. We sat nervously in the funeral home, on opposite sides of the room, occasionally exchanging bits of small talk, having no idea how to seek anything more. It was no better the next day during the graveside services for my grandfather, his father. At the church dinner afterward, I wondered whether the man I called Dad sat with us out of kinship and compassion, or merely out of obligation. I decided it didn't matter. He would return to Pennsylvania with his wife and their son, and he and I would once again go our separate ways, until another death or marriage brought us to the same place.

This bitter pattern began when I was a small child and my parents divorced. In time, I decided that refusing my heart's natural desire to have a relationship with my father was better for everyone concerned.

It made things less complicated—or so I thought. By the time I reached adulthood, the distance between us had become a way of life. I expected nothing from my dad and hoped for even less.

As I had predicted, we parted after my grandfather's funeral on civil terms and with cordial hugs that failed to turn into the loving embraces I secretly longed for. Our brief encounter served only to remind me of the void his absence had left in my life—a void I deliberately filled with preparations for the approaching holidays, a merciful distraction for the aching heart of the little girl deep inside me.

The encounter at the funeral home disappeared from my thoughts until several weeks later, when I was startled to receive an e-mail from my father. I had added our newly acquired e-mail address to our yearly holiday newsletter before mailing off Christmas cards to family and friends, but I had no idea whether he even owned a computer and never anticipated a message from him.

I stared at the short but friendly letter for what seemed like hours, trying to decide what to do. My response could lead to a dream come true or a miserable disappointment, and I wasn't sure I was ready for either. I decided to at least be polite, and that meant replying to his e-mail. So, with a deep breath and fingers shaking, I wrote a brief and cheerful reply, and quickly hit the "send" button before I had time to reconsider.

What began as a brief note from my dad and a courteous reply from me soon blossomed into a series of daily e-mails back and forth to each other. Then we started writing several times a day, and it got to the point where neither of us dared to go to bed without sending a final message to the other. We talked about what we had for dinner, our plans for the next day, what the grandkids were doing. Nothing was too silly or too mundane to include. For the first time in our lives, we were learning about each other, and we soaked in our conversations like thirsty sponges.

As our interest, familiarity, and comfort with each other grew, we approached the deeper issues that had separated us for all those years. At times the conversations were difficult, and sometimes we walked on eggshells and bit our tongues. We also spoke of anger and apologies, long-hidden hopes and fears, which set about great healing within us individually and in our relationship. The message that came through most clearly was our mutual desire to continue, and when the words got hard to hear and express, that alone saw us through.

I encouraged him to contact my brother and sisters, and, in turn, I urged them to respond to Dad. For the first time in more than thirty years, I felt we all had a chance to connect as a family, if we all made an effort.

Within months, my father and I had formed a relationship and felt a bond like we had never experienced before. Dad and his wife, Peg, and my stepbrother, David, made plans to travel to Indiana to visit us in the fall, and we planned a big get-together. In a funny twist of fate, during their visit I went into false labor with my son, Grant, and spent fifteen hours in the hospital before being sent home to wait it out. I missed most of the gathering, but when I finally arrived, our meeting was unlike any we had ever shared before. It was comfortable and joyful. We were no longer strangers. We had become friends. Parting was more difficult, and we eagerly anticipated our next chance to get together.

The e-mails continued, and phone calls became commonplace. I got to know and love my stepmother and my other brother. When Grant was born, we were proud to give him the middle name William, in honor of my dad. Word has it that Dad cried when my sister called to tell him.

Last summer, my dad came home again—this time to bid farewell to his mother, my grandmother. Once again, we gathered at a funeral home, but this time my siblings and I took our places at our father's side. He paraded us from one distant relative to another, reveling in the fact that he had the most children, grandchildren, and even great-grandchildren in the room!

When the inevitable moment to say our final good-bye to Grandma approached, I watched while each of the other cousins went with his or her parents to her casket and stood as a family. The seating arrangements had gotten a bit skewed, and we ended up several rows behind Dad. I felt sad and disappointed that, when it was our turn, we wouldn't be able to go with him. As we inched up the line and paused where my father was sitting, I surprised myself by reaching over to take his hand.

"Will you come up with us?" I asked, choking back my tears.

He looked bewildered and stumbled over his words, and finally said, "Do you need me?"

The question took me aback for a moment. In all those years and through all we had overcome, it had never once occurred to me that he would wonder if his children needed him. I had always assumed he knew.

"Yes," I replied firmly. "Yes, I do."

My dad rose from his seat, put his arm around me, and never let go. As we stood by the casket and whispered good-bye to Grandma, I buried my face in his chest and cried a million tears. In the comfort of his embrace, I cried tears at the loss of my grandmother and tears that belonged to the child within me who finally knew what it felt like to be Daddy's little girl.

It was the piece of my heart that had always been missing. No longer strangers, more than just friends . . . finally, we are family.

—*Amanda Krug*

The Table

Setting the table for two, I am struck once again by the size of this old oak giant. If my husband and I sit opposite each other, we can't even pass dishes across the wide expanse, and so my chair snuggles up against his. The remaining six chairs are gapingly empty, awaiting occasional guests and family gatherings, rare with our far-flung group. Eating at such a large table, says the feng shui book a friend gave me, breaks all the principles of positive dining. Cleaning around and underneath it bruises my hips. If we got rid of this bulky old thing and bought a more suitable drop-leaf table, we'd have room in this space for a cozy love seat, too, or a comfortable rocker and a bookshelf. Yet, I don't suggest it.

Thirty-five years ago the birth of our first child stirred longings for nicer furniture than the discount store and Salvation Army goods that had graced our first apartments. Upon attending our first-ever auction in a small South Carolina town, we bid for and won the remnants of another family's turn-of-the-century dining set: dark-oak buffet, china cabinet, sideboard, and five flimsy chairs, all for less than $100. Over time, we stripped and refinished all the pieces.

After the birth of our third child, when we moved into a house with a formal dining room, we lacked only a table. Spotting an announcement for an outdoor auction in a small town nearby, we piled our little boys into the car, hoping to find an old oak table similar in style to our other dining-room pieces. We were late arriving, and it seemed that all the tables had already been sold. But then the auctioneer asked for bids on the table he stood on. Without being able to see it clearly, we bid on it—just slightly more than we had paid for all the other dining pieces together—and won. When the auction crowd moved on to farm equipment, we examined our prize. Sturdy and solid, it was also much bigger than we had intended, with an enormous three-foot-diameter pedestal base. As my husband paled over the prospect of getting it home, the auctioneer's assistant arrived with five additional leaves.

Hours later we drove back to Kansas City in triumph, the boys in the backseat sitting atop a padded and temporarily split-in-half table, its leaves and pedestal sagging the trunk of our Ford Fairlane.

Reassembled, it remained our dining-room table through several moves for the next twenty years. And it became a fixed star in home movies and photos: High chairs pushed up against it. Boys balanced on booster seats and standing in chairs stabbing the air with fondue forks while the pot bubbled center stage. Adorned with platters of parsley-garnished turkey and standing rib roasts and homemade birthday cakes in the shapes of clowns, Snoopy, trains, and tigers. Sometimes set with crystal, silver, and china, sometimes with cartoon-figure paper plates.

There, at the old oak table, we have gathered— five or seven or nine, even eighteen or twenty. My grandparents joined us at the table, along with parents, aunts, uncles, and cousins. Once, even Santa Claus sat down for cocoa and cookies. Hosting our gourmet club, we'd drag the table into the living room and put in all the leaves. I'd starch and iron two king-size sheets, and we, alone among our friends, could seat everyone around the same table.

Twelve years ago, a move to a new house precipitated the purchase of another antique dining-room set. The old oak table—its top now so worn and scratched it must always be covered with a cloth, its base a little wobbly—was moved to the breakfast room, and its companion pieces to the family room. As our sons have set up their own households, I've offered them this set, but they've all preferred more modern goods. And truthfully, the table, even in its prime, was probably never valuable. Yet, when a friend asked for it for her daughter's apartment, I surprised myself by quickly saying no.

We've just become grandparents. I'm thinking what a great table this will be for art projects and glue guns, LEGOs and Lincoln Logs. Maybe in time we'll even need the leaves again. This old oak table is family.

—SuzAnne C. Cole

Riding the Rapids

My feet tucked deep in the fold of the inflatable raft, I brace myself as my body leans precariously over the edge. Muscles taut, adrenaline rushing, we paddle fast, faster. Every curve in the river might flip us into turbulent water. Every gushing ripple hides a jagged boulder that might crash us. Every frothing rapid conceals another danger to our heads and limbs.

Through the roar of the waves I count my children in both rafts. Seven: two I bore; five I stole. At least, I never bothered asking their mothers' permission before enfolding them into my emotional world. And now we are together, struggling to make it down the treacherous river.

We are not refugees seeking a safe shore, but adventurers on a whitewater trip. Laughing through the wild spray in our faces, we navigate in coordination, call out songs, keep the rhythm of our paddling.

Twenty years ago, Melissa and Jonathan were my first foray into collecting children, when I married their father. Jon, good-natured and accepting, was nine and, oblivious to anything but his own immediate needs, still feeding on demand. Now, behind me, ratcheting his oar in stubborn water currents, he shouts, "Hard! Hard! That's it!"

While trying to worm my way into his life, I used to race him in downhill skiing, until he was too big and too fast and left me in a swirling dust of snow. Now, I am risking limb and life in the churning waters.

Melissa was eleven and had the delighted chirp of a free bird certain that she owned the forest. I hear her cheering as we approach another rapid. Then the thunder of the water fills my head. The white-froth gush twisting behind a rock the size of my kitchen signals that the whirling undertow—the hole, as the guide calls it—could suck us to the bottom, where sharp rocks would rip our flesh. Missy and I struggled through some difficult years, which threatened our family's existence. We all came out of it better people.

Last year, Jonathan brought a wife into our family, someone more like me than like his mother. If I were to have another biological daughter, Cheryl—career-oriented, self-assured—would be the one.

Our raft heaves over and out of the rapid, and I

release my white-knuckle hold on the lip rope to stab my oar into the ferocious water. In the raft ahead of us, my oldest daughter, the soft-spoken Tomm, is singing along with my husband. Across from me in my boat, my youngest, Eden, the outdoorsy type, sends me the concerned look I used to send her when she was on the jungle gym. This is her chance to assert herself as an adult among her older siblings—and now among their three spouses.

We are tossed wildly over a series of minor rapids. Waves slam into my face. Under his red helmet, David, Melissa's husband, laughs into the wind as he navigates us. Steep granite walls rise on both sides. The upcoming passage is narrow. We paddle quickly toward a massive overhang a few feet above the water. After many years in our family, David still seems reluctant in the constellation of our mini-universe. Not today.

"Duck!" he screams over the angry noise of the river. If we don't, the rock ledge will surely decapitate us.

The ledge is now behind us. My eyes search for a napkin-sized beach on which we are supposed to put in for the night. It is there. I sigh with relief. A red-throated loon dives into a quiet pool and rises again with a silver trophy wiggling in his bill.

Tomm's husband, Barry, smiles at me. He was an easy capture. His love for his own mother, so sure-footed, preconditioned him to become my son.

Surreptitiously, as we beach it to camp for the night, he assumes some of my weight of the raft.

Exhausted, every nerve ending raw with fatigue, chilled and soggy, I am as out of my element as a wet camel and as smelly. I stumble onto the sand with the hope of sinking into its softness. But it is cold and clammy.

In a tent set up by the river-trip operators, I shuck my rubber wetsuit and the wool sweater and socks underneath. All are drenched. The suit kept me warm by locking in the water next to my skin, but now I look like a giant bleached prune.

A huge flock of geese overhead screams on its way south while I towel dry. Naked and shivering, I step in among the old oaks to crouch on a bed of leaves and try to urinate away from my ankles. Separate aches wander in the paths of my body, searching for campsites.

I slip into dry sweatpants and shirt. The flannel never felt so soft. It strokes my skin, but the chill will not leave my bones even after I am snuggled up in my down jacket. I fantasize a bubble bath to thaw my limbs. I hate being here. I hate being cold and soggy and tired, having no warm place to escape to. I hate being too old for this grueling day.

But when everyone, dry and in high spirits, gathers around a crudely made table in the field kitchen, I accept a cup of hot chocolate, and its fragrant sweetness tumbles through me.

The last rays of sun send caressing tentacles through the trees and over the water. My husband suggests we walk to the riverbank "to kiss at sunset." But at this moment, rather than cozy up in romantic rapture, I wish to capture another mental photo of my seven children, all grown, devouring their steak and potatoes with the appetite of the young.

Darkness falls. At the fire pit, tongues of flame leap high, the bursts of light dance on our faces, the smoke from burning wood mingles with the aroma of pine. Seated on fallen logs around the fire, we are a nine-point star, with multiple lines leading to and from each of the others. Some connections are drawn in hot red, some in cooler yellow. Jonathan adds a couple of logs to the fire and sends a boyish grin toward Tomm. The two of them became friends from the start; for years now, they have been keeping a running tally of their Scrabble games. Cheryl sits at my feet, exhilarated by the new experience, warmed by the food, the fire, and my affection. Melissa's arm is around Tomm, the girl who once "stole" her father but is now her sister. Eden is nestled between her two brothers-in-law, David and Barry. My husband, so full of the day and the night, can't stop moving about, and he gives each of them a high five.

We've survived the day in the untamable river. We've survived twenty years of navigating the turbulent waters of a blended family.

David pokes a long twig through a marshmallow and roasts it for me. I had vowed to have only one s'more, but as its edges shrink and curl in the fire, sending a delicious caramel smell, my taste buds tell me that more will indeed follow.

Each of us has prepared a skit, a song, or a game. As we laugh and play, I am distracted from thoughts of my sleeping bag on the plywood tent floor. I will not think about the waterlogged, cold wetsuit into which, come dawn, I will wriggle back into. These are my kids, all seven of these healthy, beautiful, and successful men and women, five of whom had not sought me out, but who are nevertheless a part of my emotional landscape, defining who I am.

—Talia Carner

Demystifying the C-Word

You can call a noncommittal man anything you like—Peter Pan, man from Mars, commitment-phobe—but I recently developed my own theory as to why so many men aren't as eager to make a commitment as most women are.

The word in any context other than the one having to do with what a woman wants from the man she loves is rife with negative connotations. "He was committed to an insane asylum." Or the onerous, "He committed a crime." You get the picture.

The plus side of this revelation is that now I can blame my so-called spinsterhood on something other than my bird legs. I like this theory.

To investigate my newfound discovery further, I looked to the library. The situation is even bleaker than I had thought. According to Mr. Webster, to commit means "to put officially in custody or confinement" or "to hand over or set apart to be disposed of." As if that isn't gruesome enough, Webster goes on to give this bone-chilling definition: "to commit something to the trash heap."

Nice. I'm thinking of granting a pardon to my past boyfriends for their unusual behavior whenever the subject of commitment came up—upon my suggestion, naturally. Who could blame them for not being thrilled with the prospect of throwing their respective lives into the garbage pile?

Okay, so as a verb the word is a bit ominous. Surely as a noun, I thought—which is, after all, the form of the word to which we women wish our men to aspire—it holds brighter promise. So my eyes scanned the page for "commitment." First there was the dreaded "official consignment by court order of a person to prison, mental hospital, etc." Hopeful that a more satisfactory definition was near, I read on. But what came next referred to what is probably men's biggest fear of all: "a financial liability undertaken." Ouch. No wonder they've never stuck around long enough to discover that I have my own 401(k).

After reading all those cupid killers, I finally found a definition that actually fit the context of a male-female relationship—kind of: "a pledge or promise to do something." How romantic. It might as well have been in fine print.

As a writer, I've always been particularly fond of

Roget's Thesaurus. When in a word jam, I often turn to my trusty orange paperback for a solution. This was certainly no exception. My old friend Roget dogged me with four poignant syllables. "Noun. See *duty.*" So much for my research in semantics. Well, I thought, at least now that I know what the culprit is, I can start wearing shorts again. The fact that my legs barely cast a shadow is no longer of consequence.

It's the C-word by definition that has given it such a bad rap. It's no wonder that the mere mention of it has the men of the world shaking in their Top-Siders. What I don't quite understand is why so few women subscribe to the male-held notion that commitment is akin to a one-way ticket to Sing Sing.

Though I haven't tried it yet, I'm fairly sure that marriage and "doing time" feel noticeably different. I would venture to say that for most single women, the word *commitment* conjures up visions of warmth, happiness, and stability. The only trash heap involved is in front of the white picket fence on Tuesday mornings.

To me, commitment means I no longer dread ringing in a New Year. I can simply look to the face beside me and rest assured that whatever follows will not have to be endured alone. It means that someone will make the midnight run for Benadryl the next time my hives show their angst-ridden faces. It means someone will hold my hand when the time comes to bury my parents. And someone will laugh at my jokes, or at least smile.

I want the person who kissed me good morning to be the same person who kisses me good night—up until and beyond the day when teeth are no longer part of our sleep-ware.

It also means I don't have to go on any more dates. Dating was fun when it was part of the growing-up process: share a meal, watch a movie, dance. Now, I find myself wondering if the stranger across the table would be a good father, if he recycles, if he can balance his checkbook.

I've reached the age where a kiss is much more than four lips touching. It's a promise of interest. And the older I get, the harder it is for me to get interested.

I want to tell a man that I'm the middle of three daughters only one more time. I'm tired of explaining that I majored in journalism but chose advertising because I like to make things up. Next summer, I'd like to play tennis with the same person I play tennis with this summer, and for summer after summer after that. How else can we know each other's vulnerabilities well enough to learn from them?

Over the last several years, I committed myself to a career. That was all well and good, but now I'm ready to dedicate my energies to something else— like, making love to my very best friend, forever.

Teaching my kid not to pull a dog's tail. Picking out a Christmas tree that will actually fit in my living room. Actually having the same living room two Christmases in a row.

And you know what? I'm convinced that most men want these things, too. It's all those negatives they associate with the C-word that makes it so scary for them.

So, this is what I've decided: When I find the man I want to grow old with, I'm going to look him straight in the eye and ask if he's ready to make a . . . game plan.

—Julie Clark Robinson

Dishwashing Therapy

I flicked on the kitchen light and immediately wished I hadn't. The kitchen was a disaster, dirty dishes everywhere. My husband laid a hand on my shoulder and whispered, "It isn't as bad as it looks." I sighed and began to fill the sink. Immediately the steam rose in spirals, and bubbles frothed at my fingertips. Weariness began to melt away as I lost myself in the rhythmic dunking, washing, rinsing, and drying of the dishes.

It's always been that way for me.

My mother-in-law often recounts the many reasons for buying a dishwasher. She says hand washing actually uses more water than does her sleek, energy-efficient model. She might be right. But I still prefer the old-fashioned way, the way my mother did it and her mother did it: with a sink full of warm soapy water, a cotton dishcloth, and my own two hands.

Some of my best childhood memories revolve around the cleanup after family dinners. As children, my brothers and I did our best to scuttle out of sight before being nabbed for dish duty. Once we were standing upon a stool in front of the sink, though, our quibbles quickly gave way to singing silly songs and listening to stories we might not have otherwise heard. Grandma fed me nibbles of dessert as she walked past, and my mother turned away, pretending not to see. When I was old enough to invite boys home for dinner, dishwashing became the ultimate test. If the young man stood and offered to help when my mother pushed back her chair at the end of a meal, he passed. If he lingered and needed to be nudged to help, he forfeited future invitations.

Before my children arrived to consume my energy, I enjoyed washing the dishes after a quiet supper with my husband. Sometimes he helped; sometimes he didn't. But there was therapy in doing something mind-numbing but essential. Lost in the ritual of soap-sudsy labor, I savored the closeness between us, thought through disagreements, and dreamed about our future.

Now that I have children, I still prefer washing dishes to almost any other chore. I can systematically avoid rooms screaming to be vacuumed. But I'll always be the first to offer to wash the dishes, even now that there are so many of them, with a family of six. I know that the therapeutic rewards will come as soon as I begin the process.

After we return from school and work, and we hungrily eat the comfort food cooked in my faithful Crock-Pot, my children help me tidy the kitchen. They swish their little hands through soapy water and tell me things in side-by-side conversations that they'd never share if asked. They interact with each other, each feeling like a useful and necessary part of our home. In a complex world full of endless challenges that have neither beginning nor end, dishwashing reminds us that not all jobs are complicated. Some are simple and easily completed—plate by plate, glass by glass, pot by pot. Order comes from chaos. If only the rest of our lives were that simple.

Some people are amazed that I have four children and no dishwasher. They don't know that I involved my children in dishwashing when their noses barely reached the counters, praising their efforts to "help Mommy," even though it initially meant more work for me. As toddlers, my children didn't consider splashing in a sink of soapy water a chore, because I hooked them into my secret enjoyment before they realized it was really work. When one child began to stutter, we washed dishes while we talked together. He slowed down and began to speak without stuttering; his speech therapist was amazed. Today, at age eleven, he still loves to wash the dishes.

When I'm left to my own solitude to scrub away the grease, it's as if I am also shedding the debris that clouds my thoughts. Solutions to problems that have eluded me all day appear and calmly settle, as if they've been waiting for me to relax and find them. Tension lifts from my shoulders; I gain some perspective. I don't want to glorify my dishwashing. It is no long soak in a bubble bath with the door locked and scented candles burning. It's not nearly as cleansing as a brisk walk in the wilderness. But in a busy life filled with activity and frustration, it's a close second.

Many of our parties have ended with our guests joyfully rolling up shirtsleeves and pitching in. As we washed dishes together, we've shared the grief and joys of our lives, sharing intimacies we wouldn't at the dinner table or in a room full of guests. We've reveled in the miracle of life as soapy hands reached out to touch a baby kicking within. We've swung tea towels over our shoulders and held each other to cry and to laugh.

Dishwashing brings joy and conversation and closeness. In the process, a kitchen thrown into disarray over the course of preparing a meal is folded back into place again.

I have never seen an automatic dishwasher do that.

—Julia Rosien

The Four Marys

I n the old black-and-white photograph with the ruffled edge, my mother is not yet thirty, and I am the sun-kissed, halo-haired child straddling her hip. Mother loves to lift the photo in the thin gold frame from its place on the mantel to show her children and grandchildren. We call it "The Four Marys," because it is a picture of four generations of women in my family, all firstborn daughters and all named Mary: my great-grandmother, my grandmother, my mother, and me. I was actually named Mary Margaret after my two grandmothers—and after all the other Marys on my mother's side of the family—but they always called me Peggy to avoid the inevitable confusion.

In the snapshot, I'm just two, and I have a studious frown on my round face. I'm staring into my cupped hand as if Tinkerbell sits there gazing up at me, and I'm pointing into my palm with my other hand. My mother remembers that just before this favorite photograph was taken, my great-grandmother had led me to her garden and let me choose any flower I wanted. Mother says it was a columbine blossom and that it captivated me so much I refused to lift my face to the camera. Columbines still charm me, looking, as they do, like exploded pastel firecrackers.

My father had gone away on a ship to fight in the Second World War. Studying the photo, you can tell the war had already had an effect on women's fashions. My great-grandmother's dark skirt is voluminous and drops nearly to her ankles. In contrast, my grandmother and mother wear tight skirts that barely cover their knees. Scarcity of fabric dictated those shorter skirts of the younger generations of women.

A high-necked dark blouse with long full sleeves and a fringed shawl in a muted floral pattern cover my great-grandmother's torso. My mother and grandmother wear skimpy blouses. Grandma's snug, low-cut top hugs her ample, matronly figure with pride, and the tatting at the collar and the edges of the sleeves, three layers deep all around, was done by her own hand. My mother wears a thin cotton voile blouse with cutwork embroidery across the bodice and at the borders of the short, scalloped sleeves.

My great-grandmother's hair, never cut and swept back into a soft bun at the nape of her neck, is dark, dark, dark, and it occurs to me for the first time that she must have dyed it. Grandma's hair is short and crimped tightly by one of the new permanent waves. Holding the photo, Mother reminds me of the fact that until just a few years earlier, her mother had never cut her hair. When she came home with a short bobbed style, carrying the four-foot braid of her hair in a paper bag, her husband was so upset that he didn't speak to her for several weeks.

My mother looks like a girl in the old Breck shampoo ads, with naturally curly hair framing her 1940s radiant complexion, painted lips, and screw-on pearl earrings. All those Breck girls looked like Raphael's angels without the extra poundage, and indeed my mother is far too thin in the photograph. Worry about my dad's safety, combined with the results of wartime rationing, account for her hipbones jutting through the fabric at the front of her skirt.

Behind the four of us in the photo are a pear tree and a flower garden. In the distance stands the farm-house where my grandmother and her five sisters were raised, and where my mother spent every summer of her youth. That flower garden between the dirt road and the house was my great-grandmother's private domain. Several times a week, she would don a wide-brimmed hat and, with a pair of shears and a broad flat basket, wander into her own special Eden. She took her time, enjoying herself and the early morning coolness as she cut enough blooms to reconstitute the many bouquets within her rambling, three-story Victorian.

My own front yard, a small city lot, also bursts with flowers. Long ago my husband and I replaced our scraggly, unsuccessful lawn with sidewalk-to-doorstep flowering plants. Each spring and summer, the low fence by the front walk disappears beneath a prolific clematis vine, and fuchsias and columbines vie with cosmos and primroses for their place in the sun. A pomegranate and a plum tree grow in the curbside strip on the far side of the sidewalk.

Not long ago, my parents visited, and my daughter (whose name is Jill, not Mary) stopped by with one of her daughters in tow.

"Oh, Mary, let's take a picture of the four generations of women in the family," suggested my father, "and you can set it next to the Four Marys."

We trooped outside and lined up in front of the garden with the purple-leafed plum tree off to one side. As we squinted into the sun, my husband fiddled with the camera's focus.

"Say cheese," my dad said from the sidelines, when everyone seemed ready.

"Wait," I said, remembering something important.

I turned to the garden, plucked a columbine blossom, and handed it to my granddaughter.

—Peggy Vincent

Camaraderie

It could have happened anywhere, but Ursula and Margrit from Switzerland, Erika from Canada, Sherry from Pennsylvania, and yours truly, Barbara, from New Jersey, found the real meaning of camaraderie in England. We met in London to complete a seven-day hike along the Cornwall coast, from Penzance to Falmouth. Three veteran hikers and two novices set out with the basic trust and optimism most women share, even though only one of us knew all four of the others. I didn't worry, because it was Ursula, one of my oldest and dearest friends, who had chosen the participants and the destination for our very first group hiking adventure—and what an adventure it was!

She'd promised a "guardian angel" to oversee our progress and delivered Stuart on the eve of our first hiking day. He met us in Penzance and provided the week's hiking map, inn itinerary, and his solemn promise to transport our luggage, and us, if necessary, to each day's destination. By hook or crook, we would all end up in Falmouth. On six of the seven days, he went on ahead of us, his compact car stuffed with suitcases. The one day a passenger usurped some luggage space, Stuart made a second trip to retrieve the left-behind bags with nary a complaint. We've never revealed which hiker bailed out that day. Loyalty reigned.

After a hearty breakfast, we'd set out each morning around nine, a compromise between the early and late risers. We assigned the "keeper" of the map, rather like an honor, since the map was encased in plastic and hung from a chain like a priceless jeweled necklace. Each woman wore it with pride, as she more or less assumed the leadership role that day. Everyone got a turn. Fairness reigned.

We studied the map scrawled with green fields, sketches, and landmarks. Though the distinctive format made sense, since we were hiking, it still surprised the beginners. To city girls, all farmlands, paddocks, and cliff paths look alike. We realized early on that my pedometer couldn't gauge our speed and pondered how to correlate the mileage with the time frames Stuart had given us. Since none of us excelled at math, we threw calculations to the wind and simply concentrated on our destination. One wrong turn, and we could be out of luck for that night's lodging, or worse, that night's dinner. We remained focused. Dedication reigned.

We felt we earned our gourmet dinners. We'd shed our hiking clothes and snazz ourselves up, just to prove the rigors of the day hadn't done permanent damage. "Aren't you ready yet?" became the hue and cry to the one who always primped the longest. But we waited, stomachs growling, and arrived in the dining room together. The first order of the evening was always a toast to our progress and the miracle that we'd ended up in the right place. We added a little fudge factor to Stuart's mileage count so we wouldn't feel badly about gorging ourselves on the wonderful meals. Each inn packed a generous lunch, but unless we happened through a small village, there wasn't an extra snack to be had. By dinner, we'd worked up an embarrassing appetite. Indulgence reigned.

The first time we got lost, we would gladly have asked directions. But since cows can't talk, we were on our own. Every day was like a treasure hunt. We climbed endless stepping-stoned walls dividing one pasture from another, hoping we were on the right track. Often, we weren't and had to scale higher walls or shimmy through fences we knew shouldn't be part of our route. One time, we sucked in our stomachs and slithered under a gate, because the surrounding wall was topped with rolls of barbed wire as far as you could see. When hiking along the cliffs, we must have gotten distracted by the gorgeous views and taken a wrong turn that led down to the beach. Suddenly, we found ourselves trudging through water and climbing over boulders, giving each other a helping hand to mount the steepest ones, until we reached the cliffs again. Whenever we veered off course, we always found a way out. Teamwork reigned.

Stuart had thrown several deadlines in our way, cautioning about high tides that could strand us on an out island if we didn't reach the mainland in time and about a ferry that we had to catch before its last run at five o'clock. We wondered if he was just trying to add to our excitement, but we didn't dare ignore him. That put extra pressure on five forty- and fifty-something women who felt pretty tuckered out after seven or eight hours of walking. But we doggedly hiked on. Courage reigned.

Everyone in our group excelled at packing. What one of us forgot, another remembered and brought spares of, including the most obscure items. By the end of the second day, we succumbed to blisters. All but one of us complained about them as we soaked our poor feet in a tub of cold water. "What's your secret?" we asked the one who'd been spared. "Moleskin," she confessed. "Don't you use it?" We'd never even heard of it. So Erika, who'd even packed scissors, became our resident nurse, cutting moleskin to soothe our blistered feet. We still laugh over the "foot" photo we took of all eight feet, forty toes, decked out in various patterns of moleskin. She opened up a whole new pain-free world for us. Caregiving reigned.

Long overdue at the end of the third day, we were grateful when we finally saw our hotel in the distance. At least, we had hoped it was our hotel. We'd been lost and rained on for what seemed like hours and had all but crawled the last few hundred yards. Closer inspection revealed a majestic entrance whose staircase loomed like Mount Everest. We trudged up. No "Rocky" runs for us. The staff graciously welcomed us, bedraggled as we were. Of all places to arrive scruffy, wet, exhausted, and starving, why did it have to be at the most elegant hotel on our itinerary? Hoping to rectify our unglamorous first impression, we all vowed to muster the energy to spruce ourselves up as best we could for dinner and then assured each other the task wouldn't be that difficult. Acceptance reigned.

For me, one of the joys of being in England was Cadbury chocolate. The others didn't seem addicted, but I'd been satisfying my sweet tooth every day from a cache I'd stored once I realized how rural and remote our route was. The farther we walked, the happier I was that I'd had the foresight to buy ahead. I must have miscalculated the number of bars, or more likely overindulged once or twice, because I depleted my supply before we reached Falmouth.

Attentive as we were to each other's needs, my friends noticed I'd gone through a day without chocolate and asked for an explanation. When I told them my supply was gone and admitted to being a pig, they burst out laughing and produced a bar one of them had planned on taking home. "No one needs this as badly as you do," they choroused. Sharing reigned.

After seven glorious days of hiking together, we rejoiced at what a harmonious group we'd turned out to be. The better acquainted we became, the more united we felt. Having only each other to rely on does that. No problems arose that we couldn't solve. No one disagreed or bickered. We were a very easy-going, fun-loving lot. Getting lost, arriving late, and suffering through bad weather and blisters hadn't brought on any temper tantrums. We joked through every "calamity" and still do when reminiscing about the trip. Laughter reigned.

As I remember it, Stuart calculated the distance from Penzance to Falmouth at about sixty-five miles. However, the pedometer I faithfully wore clocked our final mileage at eighty-two miles. Our maximum daily output was fifteen and a quarter miles, but most days averaged around ten miles. We'd done a lot of wandering and exploring, so getting lost wasn't the only reason for the discrepancy. Even if it had been, we'd had fun doing it. Perseverance reigned.

Stuart joined us for dinner on the last evening of the hike. When we told him some of the high points of our adventure, he laughed with us. Then, he turned serious and told us how proud of us he was. We were pretty close to tears, until Ursula saved the day. Being the eternal optimist and having complete confidence in our success, she'd made up hiking diplomas for the whole group, certifying that at least sixty-five miles (plus several planned and unplanned detours) of hiking on the Cornwall Coastal Path from Penzance to Falmouth in England had been mastered by each member of the group. She'd had our names printed on them with spaces for our fellow hikers to sign and even a space for Stuart, our "coach." They are treasured souvenirs. Thoughtfulness reigned.

In my search for heartfelt friendship, unselfish teamwork, steadfast unity, and unconditional support, I learned that it isn't "location, location, location." It's people, people, people, and most specifically, women, women, women!

—*Barbara Nuzzo*

Legend of the Perfect Girlfriend Girl

nce upon a time, I had an amazing talent. I was able to morph into the perfect woman instantly, given the proper provocation—the proper provocation being a handsome man gainfully employed; no previous convictions; reasonably literate; interested in wine, music, museums, me . . . you know, a marrying man.

One, "Can I call you?" from Mr. Marrying Man, and I immediately began to spin around à la Lynda Carter in *Wonder Woman*. Sparks would fly, my theme song would play, and when the smoke cleared, I would be magically transformed into Her. You know which Her I'm talking about. You may have seen her in a restaurant or known her in high school, or maybe you, too, are one of Her. I am talking about Perfect Girlfriend Girl. *Ta-daa!* The girlfriend who never argues, never complains, and never shows any outward displeasure about anything her prospective husband might do or fail to do.

One of Perfect Girlfriend Girl's amazing disguises is Girl Without Bodily Functions. I am sure you are familiar with her as well. She doesn't burp, pee, stink, or have unwanted body hair. The mythical tale about the one time I maybe possibly farted was like an urban legend: Someone knew someone who knew someone who was there when it had supposedly happened but who hadn't actually witnessed it.

Of course, all of this is training for the day when Perfect Girlfriend Girl evolves into Wonderful Wife Woman, who possesses even greater superhuman powers. Those powers are inclusive of, but not exclusive to, making five-course gourmet dinners, bearing brilliant kids, keeping a feng shui home while earning a six-figure income, and being the perfect arm piece for black-tie affairs.

Why, you might ask, did I put myself through such torture? Why not be myself and let the chips fall where they may? I'll tell you why . . .

It began when I was about sixteen years old. I was in the kitchen cooking with my grandmother. I think we were making home fries. Anyway, Grandma, a wonderfully, if sometimes scathingly, candid woman who was raised in the South, eyed my potato-peeling technique and proclaimed with all certainty, "Oh, baby! You'll never get a husband peeling a potato like that!"

Now, in retrospect, I realize that my grandmother's notion that my ability to find and acquire a husband was closely tied to, if not directly reliant upon, my proficiency at peeling a potato was a little far-fetched, if not (sorry, Grandma) completely nuts. But I was sixteen and had little experience in these matters. My grandmother was at least three times my age and had managed to snag the greatest man who ever lived—my grandfather. So, maybe there was some validity, if only a smidgen, in what she had to say.

From that moment on, I picked my grandmother's brain for other tried and true ways of winning a man's heart. I mean, since I had already skunked the potato-peeling thing, I might as well find out what else I needed to brush up on. Because being a husbandless woman is a fate worse than death, right?

Being able to pinpoint this experience as being the root of my neurosis is what therapists call a breakthrough, or what Oprah might call an Aha! moment. Now, don't get me wrong. I am not blaming my grandmother for her advice. She was, God love her, giving me the best strategy she had for the kind of hand-to-hand combat that finding a good husband involved. These pearls of wisdom had probably worked for her, and her mother had probably bestowed them on her while she was improperly peeling a potato. I also understand why it worked for her.

You see, my grandmother grew up in the late 1930s and early 1940s. It was a different world then, a time when men were gentlemen, and a chiffon scarf was a necessity for every outfit. Though women had won the right to vote in the recent past, the best thing a girl could aspire to was meeting the man of her dreams, getting married, having a couple of rug rats, and dying a nonviolent death, all while perfectly coifed.

The funny thing is, no matter how many times we see a female CEO of a major company or watch *The Joy Luck Club,* there is a part of us that believes our worth as a woman is still tied to three things: our beauty, our ability to cook, and our ability to have children. This is not because we don't know any better than to believe such baloney. It is because we're unwilling to take the risk that there may be so much as a grain of truth to all that drivel. So, we buy into the lies and don our superhero capes. At least, that's what some of us do, and I did once upon a time.

But I am here to tell you . . . there is no knight in shining armor galloping about on his trusty horse in search of the perfect girl who fits the glass slipper. There is no guaranteed formula for finding a mate any more than there is a right or wrong way to peel a potato (thank God!). And twisting yourself into a pretzel to fit what you think is someone else's notion of who and how you should be . . . well, it doesn't work, and it just isn't worth it. Sooner or later, you forget to pick up your magic cape at the cleaners, or the magic dust that has been blurring your vision finally clears and you see the troll you'd mistaken for a prince.

As I have learned through many a painful lesson, it is better to be whole and alone than to be a fragmented version of yourself with someone. Man or no man, kids or no kids, whether she cooks like Martha Stewart or burns microwave popcorn, every woman deserves happiness and success just the way she is. So, ladies, let it rip. Let your hair down. Let it be. And let's all tell Perfect Girlfriend Girl to get real and to go take a hike.

—Shaun Rodriguez

The Trip to Plentiful

Two years ago, my mother bought a small log cabin in the woods of Cloudcroft, New Mexico, where she could work on her oil paintings and get away from the Texas heat.

That summer, Mom called us to report a beautiful 70 degrees in the mountains. "Why don't you come for a visit?" she asked.

My husband couldn't take time off work, but that didn't stop our seven-year-old daughter, Mindy, and me. Leaving him behind with the dog, five cats, and the refrigerator door plastered with instructions, we traveled from sea level to an altitude of more than 9,000 feet to join Mom for a two-week respite.

Mom picked us up at an airport in nearby Alamogordo, and after exchanging hugs, I prepared for a pleasant country drive to the cabin. As we made our way up the mountain, the four-lane highway narrowed to a thin two-lane road bordering a steep canyon wall. Lovely fields of wildflowers, apple orchards, and pine trees began to appear. Mom pulled off the road at a rest area so we could stretch our legs. Mindy pointed to cliffhangers rappelling from a crag into a ravine. The view was breathtaking.

When we resumed our journey, black rain clouds had begun to gather around the mountaintop.

"Is that where we're headed?" I asked, pointing to the smoky-looking ridge.

"Yes. I hope we can make it up there before the afternoon rains begin."

I shifted nervously in the velvety seat of the 1989 Crown Victoria. Mom reached into her purse, extracted a lighter, and lit a cigarette. As we inched higher and higher into the mountains, dark fog seemed to swallow up the car.

"Hang on tight, girls!" Mom said, as the car suddenly spun around a sharp curve.

The unpaved road leading to the cabin was steep. The eight-cylinder engine roared as the car catapulted over large rocks in the muddy road—and as my life passed before my eyes.

The tumultuous ride came to an abrupt end, like being thrown from a bull in a rodeo.

"We're here!" Mom said. "What do you think?"

My brain was a milkshake; I couldn't think.

"I need to go to the bathroom," Mindy whined,

bouncing up and down in the backseat.

"There's no bathroom," Mom announced. "But there's an outhouse up the hill."

The cabin was nestled at a 45-degree angle on the side of the mountain, and a splintery toilet was located several yards above the cabin. The car door swung open, waving hello with the wind.

"At least we'll get some exercise," I said, as Mindy and I started up the hill.

Loose pine needles made for a slick trail. Mindy took a few steps, whirled around, and landed smack-dab on her fanny.

"Are you okay?" I helped her to her feet and began to brush off her backside. A gooey substance stuck to my hand. "*Peee-uuu-wee!* What's that smell?" I asked, examining my hand.

"It's raccoon poop," Mom said from a distance, knowing from experience, not having to come any closer.

In less than five minutes at Mom's cabin, I already had a big mess on my hands—literally.

"Grab that bucket, and we'll bring up water from the well to clean her up." Mom said.

"From the well?" I echoed in disbelief.

Not only was there no bathroom, there was no running water! Mom's cabin was more rustic than I had expected. And that was only the beginning of the startling discoveries to come.

Mother had been accustomed to a life of luxury. So, it surprised me to see her actually enjoying the hard work that accompanied mountain living. And when I entered the cabin, it was apparent that leaving civilization had roused her artistic talents: Several beautiful oil paintings were propped up around the room drying. It had been years since Mom had felt like painting.

The sun disappeared behind the trees, and the evening grew cold. We built a fire in the iron stove on the porch. Peculiar sounds seemed to magnify as evening fell.

"What's that noise, Mommy?" Mindy asked and crawled into my lap.

Masked faces began peeping up around the porch. The light from the fire illuminated their shiny black noses and button eyes.

"Oh, that's Mrs. Raccoon and her five little ones," my mother said cheerfully. "Don't worry; they won't bother you."

At bedtime, Mindy and I bunked upstairs in the A-frame's loft. Mindy awoke at 1:00 A.M. and asked if I would take her to the outhouse.

"Now?" I moaned, searching for the flashlight. I put on my shoes, bundled Mindy up, and held her hand as we began the hike up the hill.

The light from the crescent moon created long, thin shadows across the landscape. Stars hung like crystal beads in the sky. Suddenly, the silence was shattered when a pinecone struck the metal roof of the cabin. Mindy scrambled into my arms. "Are there bears up here, Mommy?"

"Don't ask me that right now," I replied, shivering.

"I don't really need to go potty now. Let's go back."

I didn't argue. We turned around and hightailed it back to our bunk.

A few hours later, the morning sun glistened on the windows. We awoke to bees buzzing in the walls of the cabin. Mindy said it sounded like a dentist's office and covered her head with a blanket to sleep a little longer. Mother cooked bacon and eggs over an open fire, while I brought up water from the well and made coffee. Squirrels chattered and scolded from treetops, and brightly colored hummingbirds darted from tree to tree. There were signs of wildlife all around: deer tracks, raccoon remnants, even bear scratch marks on the trees.

"This is God's country," Mom said proudly. "God's beautiful country."

After several days, we drove into the village of Cloudcroft to buy groceries. The village looked like a scene out of a western movie. A man offered tourists a ride on his horse and buggy for three dollars. Mindy and I took a tour of the town, while Mom stayed behind to visit friends.

On the way back to the cabin, we stopped to fill up the car with gas at a quaint country store. Mindy tugged at my sleeve and pointed. "Look at that big dog!"

I looked in the direction Mindy was pointing. "That's not a dog! That's a wolf!"

"She's the store owner's pet," my mother said.

The lanky animal had a beautiful thick tail and silky coat with streaks of white and gray. She watched us through intense golden eyes. The owner stood with Mindy, so she could pet the wolf while I took pictures.

It was an experience I'll never forget. We lived like *Grizzly Adams*. We bathed in a bucket, washed dishes and clothes in a bucket, collected firewood in a bucket, and—after that first night—made an emergency Porta Potti of a bucket.

We returned home to my husband with stories of the mountains and its creatures, and tales of an enchanting cabin and its not-so-charming outhouse.

"How does your mother survive without the necessities?" he asked.

I thought for a moment and then said, "For Mom, solitude and nature are necessities. Perhaps she feels the same as the famous American painter Albert Pinkham Ryder, who said, 'The artist needs but a roof, a crust of bread, and an easel, and all the rest God gives in abundance.'"

—*Gina Tiano*

NAZIK

The Truth about Dreams

I'll never forget that "very important meeting" with my guidance counselor during my senior year of high school. I gladly and dutifully shared my aspirations, and was looking forward to hearing his life-changing advice on how best to achieve my educational and occupational goals for the future. He proceeded to tell me that I was not college material and that, based on my academic history, "possibly a nice secretarial school" would be more my league. His advice did change my life, though not in the way he expected—because I did not follow it. I didn't even consider it. By trying to put limitations on my future, he made me even more determined to pursue a college degree and a career of my choosing. And I had no interest in, and no intention of, becoming a secretary.

At that moment in my eighteenth year, I took

charge of my destiny. I decided what kind of a college I wanted to attend—one that was small, personal, and would foster my enthusiasm and varied interests. I searched through many catalogs and resources until I found the one for me: Endicott Junior College, then a women-only college in Beverly, Massachusetts. When I visited Endicott, it felt like home, and my choice was made. It was the only college I visited, applied to, and was interviewed by. Boy, did that make heads spin! "How can you do that? Are you crazy?" It was a response I would hear often for the rest of my life.

I was accepted at Endicott for the fall semester and immediately knew it was the right school for me. After studying subjects ranging from English and early childhood education to psychology and art, I graduated with an associate's degree in advertising—and on the dean's list. I was elected the vice president of student government, and I headed the student concerns committee. I also was a member of Shipmates, a welcoming committee for future students, and I made friends for life. So much for not being college material!

Because advertising is a broad field, I decided to specialize in graphic design and to continue my education at the local community college. After earning another associate's degree, this one in art, I transferred to one of the state universities. I was determined to get my bachelor's degree—and did, while holding two part-time jobs.

With my academic career firmly in hand, I began to think seriously about where I wanted my education to take me. Where did I want to work? What specifically did I want to do as a profession? What kind of work environment did I want? Where did I want to live, to get up every morning and go to work every day and come home every night? My answer was always the same, the place I had looked forward to visiting every year with my family—Disney World, in Orlando, Florida.

After much contemplation, my boyfriend and I decided to get married the following spring and move from family, friends, homes, and jobs in Connecticut to Florida. Heads wagged and eyes rolled, and people said, "You can't just move to Florida!" or "Why Florida?" I would smile and say that I wanted to work in Disney's design department. "Well, now, wouldn't we all, sweetie. You know, you just can't have everything you want." Why not? I thought to myself. I had grown up with Disney movies and books and songs telling me to follow my dreams and to wish upon stars and to find my Prince Charming. I'd found my prince, so I was going for the rest of my dream.

We arrived in Florida, and shortly after, I started working at the LEGO Imagination Center in downtown Disney. It wasn't the design department, yet, but I knew that everything I did was a small stepping-stone to where I wanted to be. I submitted my resume to the design department, continued working hard at the LEGO center, and after ten months I received an invitation to interview with the Disney design group. My hopes were high, but I did not expect a miracle. After all, I had almost no design experience. What I did have was education (thank you very much), my spirit, and an interview for the job of my dreams. In a large conference room in front of fifteen to twenty art directors, project managers, and designers, I gave it my best shot. I impressed even myself, and just being in that building and having the opportunity to present my qualifications to that prestigious group of people bolstered my sense of self-confidence.

I didn't get the job, not that job, not yet. They told me to get some hands-on experience and then try again, and that they would hold on to my file. I believed them, and I did just that. I went to work for a magazine. As I sharpened my design skills, I found a new passion: writing. With my eye always on the goal of one day designing for Disney, I worked my way up to assistant art director at the magazine.

About a year and a half later, during the same week, I received four exciting phone calls: one from Nickelodeon, one from Harcourt-Brace Publishing, one from the Disney design group—and one from my doctor's office saying that I was pregnant with identical twin girls. I interviewed with each of the companies. That time at Disney, I met with only ten people, and they seemed surprised at how much I had grown professionally. I received job offers from all three places, and began a freelance art position with Disney the following Monday morning.

Not surprisingly, my boss at the magazine was displeased with my short resignation notice. Perhaps it would have been less of an unpleasant shock had my former boss known how long I had waited for this moment and how hard I had worked to make it come true. There was no way I could delay for even a day the realization of a lifetime dream. My greatest pleasure was when I called home to say, "Mom and Dad, guess what? I *did* it! Now, when people ask you how I'm doing, you just tell them, Extraordinarily well! Living in warm weather, married to an incredible man, working at her dream job at the Disney design group, and expecting twin daughters in February!'"

I am now a stay-at-home mommy with new dreams. I want healthy, happy children; to be a great role model for my girls; and maybe to write a novel. I want to live my life my way, to love and laugh, to approach each day with an open mind. I have come to realize that only I hold the key to my happiness, and the best for me is yet to come.

One day, when my little girls tell me that they

want to sing the national anthem at an NHL hockey game, to paint a picture that will hang in a museum, to dance on Broadway, to ice-skate in the Olympics, or to do something I haven't even conceived of for them, I will tell them they can do anything their little hearts desire. You can bet I'll be right there, doing everything in my power to support them in making it happen. Because I know: Dreams really do come true.

—*Shannon Pelletier-Swanson*

T Roses

The two men spoke with an easiness that con-
trasted sharply with the setting.

"So, after you left your position as chief of police
here, you joined the United Nations?" Ed said from
the chair next to the hospital bed of his blind and
gravely ill friend.

"No, I went to work for the federal government,
the Foreign Service Agency, helping other countries
upgrade their police forces."

"I knew that you two had lived in Greece and
Brazil," Ed said. "And I seem to remember that you
were in Libya, too—or was it Liberia?"

"Both," T chuckled.

"Jet-setters, eh? Paris? London? Monaco?" Ed
teased.

"Hardly! We worked mainly in Third World
countries plagued with coups and chaos, where

police forces had been unable to protect the lives of innocent citizens: Guam, El Salvador, Panama, Colombia, British Guiana, South Vietnam."

"And Carla went with you to all those places?" Ed asked.

"Not only did she go with me, she absolutely charmed the people. Invited them into our home. Made deep friendships. We still get Christmas cards from all over the world," T said.

"I see."

"Ed, she's been the best part of my life. Every step of the way, she's been right there, and she's been at my bedside with the heart attacks and the strokes. She even cuts up the meat on my plate now that I can't see it anymore. She leads me back when I get lost going from our dining room to the living room. And she does it without sneering or acting like she's getting tired of the old man."

"Yeah, I remember. We couldn't make heads or tails out of what you were saying after that last stroke. But Carla knew," Ed said.

"So, you understand then . . ."

"I understand, man. I understand."

At three in the morning, Carla finally stumbled home from the hospital. Drained, she sat at the edge of their bed to take off her shoes and then fell back, too exhausted to undress or even to crawl under the covers.

She slept until after ten o'clock the next morning—waking for the first time in a world without T. Just when he had finally begun to rally after his most recent heart attack, another massive stroke had done him in. It had taken both calamities to still that strong-willed and tough, but gentle, man.

It took Carla two hours to leave their bed, so empty now without him, knowing he'd never return to her side. Weeping under a cascade of warm water, she felt refreshed enough after a shower to get dressed and get moving. She got as far as the living room, and drew the blinds before sitting down in the shadows.

Reluctantly, she reached for the envelope T had left on the coffee table between their chairs. He'd given her strict instructions to open it once he was gone. The sight of her name written in the awkward, uphill letters he had reverted to when his vision faded tore her apart. With trembling fingers, she eased the paper out of the envelope and was surprised to see the clarity of the handwriting, to see that it was not T's. Though the letters looked familiar, she couldn't place who had written this for him. But the squiggled signature at the bottom was definitely her husband's.

Sighing, Carla started to read what looked to be a list. And then she burst out in laughter choked with tears. T had been at peace with what was happening, and he had told her so, as he always had, in humor.

The list began: "If my body is to be cremated, make sure I'm really dead first."

The rest was a compilation of reminders of important papers and items that he wanted her to see to. This was followed by a detailed outline of his funeral service. It was so like him to take on the burden of the planning, to ease her sorrow now. He had requested a service of simple dignity, but one laced with the sardonic humor that he'd always used to deal with tough situations.

The tears again rose of themselves, and just then, there was a light tap at her front door. "Oh, no," she thought. It was too soon. She didn't feel up to facing anyone. Carla's first thought was to pretend she wasn't home. Then, hastily wiping her eyes, she took a deep breath and rose to look between the slats of the blinds.

Outside, she saw Ed's canary-yellow Beetle parked at the curb, and then Ed scurrying down the front walk.

"Ed?" she called from the door, but he merely waved.

"You okay?" he called.

She nodded. Ed waved again and got into his VW and drove away.

A long, white florist's box stood propped against the doorframe. It was tied with gold-edged red ribbon like the one T had sent her on their anniversary.

Carla felt the tears again as she brought the box inside the house and closed the door.

She fumbled with the ribbon, unwilling to cut it with scissors. At last it slid off the end of the box, and she lifted the lid to look inside at a dozen perfect long-stemmed white roses. Nestled against the white satin ribbon was a tiny card with scrawled letters she could barely decipher. It was her husband's handwriting.

"Thanks," it said, "Love, T."

—Mary Jane Nordgren

The Rising of the Sun

I was asleep when I felt him touch my arm and shake me. I tried to ignore him, but he was persistent . . . as usual. I rolled over and glared sleepily at him.

"What do you want?" I snapped.

His face was hidden in darkness, but I could sense his excitement. His whole body tensed with it.

He whispered hoarsely, "Wanna watch the sun come up?"

I did want to, very much. So I got dressed in my sleeping bag, while he heckled me, whispering: "Who wants to look at you, anyhow? I can't see you. Who'd look? What do you got worth lookin' at? Hell, I could iron a shirt on your chest."

And so he continued until I squirmed free of the sleeping bag. Taking my hand in his, he led me past the other sleeping bags and toward the tent flap.

Climbing over our sisters was easy. Climbing over Mama was nothing short of life threatening. She was small but tough, and if she caught us . . .

Once outside the tent, the hugeness of the mountain overwhelmed us to stillness and silence. He and I stood, side by side, gazing at the dark purple giant, listening to birds calling from dark, shadowy trees.

After a few minutes, he turned to me and whispered, "Let's go!"

Mel ran in a crouch, Indian-style, so I had to run that way, too, hurrying behind him through the trees that scraped and scratched at my face, skin, and clothes. Being a boy, Mel didn't care about scraped skin and snagged clothes. My gender demanded a more acute sense of personal damage. Eventually, I would learn to worry about things like calories, suntans, and flyaway hair. But that early morning in the Blue Ridge Mountains, my only aim was to keep up with my most revered hero, who cared not one whit about the condition of my apparel or whether my arms were bleeding. Had I uttered even the slightest hint of a complaint, I would have been accused of being a *girl* (what could be worse?) and sent back to the tent.

Eventually he found a path, and we walked it beneath the soft moonlight. Mel warned me about bears, and when he heard me swallow hard, he reminded me that he was part Indian. It did not occur to me to suggest that, if he was part Indian, then I must also be part Indian. All I knew was that his declaration of kinship with the Cherokee tribe made him impervious to things like ax murderers, escapees from insane asylums who brandished hooks where their hands should be, bullies who liked to hurt little girls, and now, obviously, bears as well. If I stayed close to Mel, no evil could befall me, and my love for him made my chest hurt.

We found an outcropping of rocks, and in the near-total blackness scrambled onto it and perched ourselves at the very edge. Thus situated, dangling straight out over the Shenandoah Valley, which slept peacefully thousands of feet directly beneath us, my brother and I watched the sun ease its way over the Blue Ridge.

Pale and delicate, the day seemed rather shy when it was new, stepping politely in our direction as if in proper greeting. A summer lady she was—a bashful, understated Southern belle cloaked in finery. She wore pink and the most demure shade of violet with an orange sash about her waist. Then, without warning, she tossed off her frail pinks and violets and flung herself at us all wrapped in daring blue and red and purple. I laughed, and Mel laughed. He whistled between his fingers, and I clapped my hands as we both swung our legs energetically back and forth over the rocky, murderous drop into the valley.

Then the day threw off her colors and stood

naked before us, wearing nothing but the sun, and she seemed not nearly so pretty without her lavish wardrobe. Mel and I lost interest in her and slumped wearily against each other. He would droop forward, then snap himself awake. Then I would sigh, crumple sleepily toward the tip of that rock, and come suddenly awake again.

In the end, he and I curled up together like two kittens and slept wrapped in each other for warmth. Mama found us well over an hour later, and we got into terrible trouble, Mel worse than me. Being part Indian didn't do him a bit of good when Mama was yelling things like, "You are older than she is! I don't expect you to act like that! I expect you to take care of her!"

If you have never been spanked with a wooden spoon, it is useless trying to describe it. Let me assure you, however, that the impact of a small, slender piece of wood on a quivering set of buttocks is something one remembers clear into adulthood.

Then Mama turned to me. She was angry beyond angry and demanded to know what I had learned from this experience. I answered right away, for I had been paying close attention and knew full well what had been shown to me.

"I am like daytime, Mama," I told her. "I am scared at first, but if I know you like me, I will show you all my colors. And if I am sure you love me, I will take off all my clothes and dance!"

She stared at me, speechless, so I figured I could go and hurried off toward camp before she remembered what she'd intended to do. As I passed my brother, I heard him mutter, "Dance with no clothes on? What a dumb-ass thing to say. Who the hell would look at you anyway?"

But I was too happy, and he could not make me mad. Mel could be part Indian if he wanted to be. I was part Dawn and that was much, much better.

—*Camille Moffat*

The Christmas Box

Every year, for as long as I can remember since moving away from Dexter, Michigan, the small town in the Midwest where I grew up, the Christmas box has arrived in the early weeks of December. It brings not only gifts of the holiday but also gifts of the spirit, those precious memories of my childhood that take me back to a time when life was simple and sweet.

The box is heavy, wrapped in brown paper and strongly secured with strapping tape. No longer addressed in the rounded handwriting of my mother, so familiar from her letters written to me over the years, the label is now written in my father's hand.

Inside the box are small, hand-wrapped gifts for the family—kitchen towels, a bottle of Old Spice aftershave, and chocolate-covered cherries. It contains the familiar fruitcake, which nobody ever eats, and gifts for the children that, regardless of their age, seem stuck in the time warp of toys for ten-year-olds. My father becomes thriftier as he ages, and, in addition to the toys, sends the children $10 one year, $5 the next, then a dollar bill, and finally three quarters taped to an index card.

The sweetest gifts in the Christmas box are those that come unwrapped—the gifts of the heart, which, in their sameness each year, touch my soul and take me home again. The first of these is a bag full of Michigan leaves! Carefully I spread out the colorful, parchment-thin leaves. I admire the silhouette of their delicate veins when I lift them to the light. The leaves take me back to Michigan autumns, when as a child I raked the leaves into huge piles and jumped into the haystack-shaped lumps at the side of the road. I remember the smell, the crunch, and the feel of the leaves covering me as I lay hidden in my nest. That delicious cozy feeling of being safe in my world of leaves lingers with me now as I inhale their deep musty fragrance. When I grew tired of playing in the leaves, my father set them on fire, and I threw in horse chestnuts from the old tree in the backyard, the one next to my clubhouse, and waited for them to pop. Long after I went to bed, I smelled the trails of smoke in the air and heard an occasional chestnut exploding. As I reminisce, I can almost feel the heat of the fire on my face as the dry leaves crackle and snap in the flames.

Then there is the bittersweet: a brilliant fiery orange plant with berries that burst out of their casings like popcorn. My father gathers it each year along dusty country roads. Dried and bundled together with thick rubber bands, it reminds me of my mother, who kept bunches of bittersweet in her cobalt blue vases on the mantel, where they brightened the long gray days of winter. In the spring, she replaced them with pussy willows, nature's first hint that winter's end was near. Until her death, she made sure to include a bunch of bittersweet in the Christmas box, and my father continues the custom. I arrange the dried bouquet in my mother's blue vase, where it creates a splash of color on my own mantel.

The Christmas box always contains a jar of Sanders Hot Fudge sauce, which is so rich and heavenly I tell my young children it is poison, and then eat it in secrecy in the bathroom, the only private place in the house. Sanders Hot Fudge reminds me of going on shopping trips in Detroit with my parents in the 1950s. Since we lived in a small town, we made a great expedition out of going to the city. My father couldn't keep up with the rigors of shopping, so after an hour or so, he headed for the car with his newspaper, coffee, and a doughnut while my mother and I roamed the shopping center. If it was Christmas season, I begged my father to hold off on the trip until the weather was cold and snowy and there was a Santa Claus on every corner. I loved the large crowds, the big department stores and their window decorations, carols playing, and the Salvation Army ringing bells on the street corners. I especially liked the feel of going from warm stores into the icy wind and snowflakes outside. Our trips included a visit to Sanders Soda Fountain, where we waited for an available spot at the counter so that we could sit on the black leather stools and order hot fudge sundaes for a quarter, along with tall glasses of ice water. Sundaes were served in silver trays with paper lining and contained round balls of pure French vanilla ice cream with warm fudge sauce spooned over the top. No whipped cream or cherry was added to mask the wonderful taste. As I open the Christmas box and feel the familiar shape of the glass jar of fudge sauce in its Christmas wrapping, I can taste the warm chocolate even before I open the jar.

And what would the box be without Michigan apples! My father thinks of ingenious ways to wrap them for shipping. Sometimes they are wrapped in foil, sometimes in plastic bags, and sometimes in newspaper. My father attaches little labels to each apple as to kind and use: "Red Delicious, good for eating"; "Roman Beauty, use for cooking"; "Macintosh, soft apple"; "Jonathan, keeps well." Of course, they make the box weigh a ton. Each Christmas when

I receive the notice of a package at the post office, I rush to pick it up, and when the fragrance of apples fills the post office as the heavy package is carried out, I know it is the Christmas box. The tree-ripened Michigan apples from home make my box complete.

This year my father reminds me that he is getting older and hints that perhaps he will not send the Christmas box and will send money for a few gifts instead. Oh, the pain in my heart. "Not this year, Daddy, please, not this year," I murmur to myself. This year has been particularly hard, with more than its share of sorrow and loss. I want this sameness, this consistency in my life, to hang on to for just a while longer; this belief, for a moment, that some things never change.

And joy of joys! On December 6, a carton arrives. When the carrier hands me the package, I know instantly it is the Christmas box. The familiar handwriting and the Dexter Post Office label do not tell me anything I do not already know. After I drag the heavy box into the house, slit open the tough tape, and lift the lid, the familiar fragrance of apples fills the air, and tears run down my cheeks. I am wrapped in the warmth of my family's love. My father has found a way to once again bring me home for Christmas.

—Gail Balden

Julie's Gift

Several years ago, I had a good job that paid well. I worked with great people, and I liked the company. Then, one day, I realized that I wasn't really enjoying the work; I was merely content. Cows are content, I reasoned; people shouldn't be.

That was when I decided it was time for a change. I pulled out my resume, updated it, and applied for a promotion in another department. The following week, I went on vacation to Ireland and forgot about my job. When I returned, I had a voice-mail message from Human Resources saying that I was scheduled for an interview that afternoon.

On my lunch hour, I pored over a magazine filled with interviewing tips, all promising to help land the perfect job. I read about the hidden messages of body language, how to dress for success, and the absolute best responses to interview questions. To me, the advice sounded nothing like what anyone would actually do in a real job interview. Or was I that far out of touch? I kept my appointment and hoped for the best.

The interviewer was a barrel-chested man who wore bright red suspenders over his oxford shirt. He conducted the interview from his leather swivel rocker, while I sat in a small wooden chair at the foot of his mahogany desk. He tented his fingers when he asked each question, then scribbled on a piece of paper after my response. During the first half-hour, he covered the expected questions about my work history, my education, and my goals. He nodded a lot and smiled a few times, and I began to relax and feel more confident.

Then, peering over his bifocals, he folded his hands beneath his chin and said, "Now, here is your final question: What event or accomplishment in your life has made you the most proud?"

An image of Bert Parks holding a microphone in front of a Miss America contestant flashed before my eyes. This is the Big One, I thought. Depending on how I answered this question, I would either get the nod and parade down the runway with an armful of roses or fake a smile and act like a gracious loser.

Pausing for a moment, I wondered if I should follow the magazine suggestions or go with my instincts and be myself. Forget the magazine, I decided. If I was going to work with this guy, I wanted to let him know the kind of person I really was.

"Actually, my proudest moment wasn't anything I did," I said, "But something my daughter did about ten years ago."

Then I told him the story of Julie's gift.

Many years earlier, when my husband worked for the Army, he was transferred overseas. After we'd lived in Germany for about a year, my brother called from St. Louis with the news that my father had passed away. Like most men of his generation, Dad managed the money, while Mom took care of the house. After Dad died, my brother took over Mom's finances.

Shortly after my husband, my two children, and I returned to Germany following Dad's funeral, my brother called again. He'd been going over Mom's paperwork and found out that she wouldn't receive her benefits for several months. Until then, she would have to live off her meager savings.

At the supper table that evening, I told my husband I was going to send Mom some money. Our conversation was cut short by a phone call. A neighbor wanted Julie to baby-sit.

At fourteen, Julie was always looking for ways to earn spending money. She had recently started buying some of her own clothes, and it seemed as though she discovered a new favorite musical group each week whose recordings she just had to have.

The following morning, she handed me an envelope.

When I looked at the address and saw it was for my mom, I gave her a big hug. I told her how proud I was of her for taking the time to write her grandma. She shrugged and walked out the door for school, no mushy stuff for that kid.

A week later my brother called. He thanked me for the check and told me how Mom cried when she got Julie's letter. I told him how tickled I was that Julie had written the letter without my suggesting it.

Then he told me he wasn't talking about the letter, but what was inside. Julie had sent her grandma the five dollars she had earned baby-sitting. In her letter, she told her grandma to spend it on whatever she needed.

I paused during the interview and looked up. "I know that isn't really a job accomplishment, but that's what I'm most proud of in my life."

The interviewer had put down his pen and was no longer writing.

"I'm sorry," I said. "Whenever I tell anyone that story, I get carried away. What made me proud was not only what Julie had done, but also that she didn't tell anyone. If my brother hadn't called, I probably would never have known."

He stood up and shook my hand. "I think we've covered everything. You should hear from Human Resources in a week or so—one way or another."

On the way back to my office, I chided myself for revealing something so personal to a stranger and figured that was one promotion I would never get.

As promised, a week later, Human Resources called. The job was mine if I still wanted it.

A few years ago, just before my boss's retirement, the subject of my interview came up, and I asked him why he selected me. He told me that all the candidates were well qualified, but after hearing about what made me most proud, he decided I was the type of employee he wanted working in his organization.

This time, I was the recipient of Julie's gift. Once again, her simple act of love given from the heart so many years before had paid off in dividends.

—*Donna Volkenannt*

The Wrong-Number People

hree months after returning to Scottsdale, Arizona, from Scotland, my seventy-five-year-old mother-in-law, Vera, was diagnosed with cancer. She was given only a few months to live. Numb with shock, my husband, Charlie, desperately searched the Internet for medical trials and remedies to extend the life of his mother, the rock of his life.

Vera immediately began an aggressive treatment program. Despite her age and worsening condition, her doctors determined that removing her cancerous kidney was her only hope for survival. During surgery, however, the doctors discovered that the cancer had metastasized to her liver. So, throughout the postoperative recovery period, Vera received chemotherapy to destroy the cancer cells in her liver. Exhausted from the disease and the aggressive treatments, Vera slept twenty-two hours a day for most of those first two months.

When Vera was awake, though, she was comforted by a blooming friendship with a couple she had met quite by accident only a year earlier. Thinking she was calling her cousin Shirley in Scotland, Vera had misdialed and reached the number of Margaret and Duncan. They ended up talking at length. But it didn't end there. Additional "phone visits" followed, and then Vera fulfilled a lifelong wish and crossed the great pond to Scotland. My husband, our daughter, and I went with her.

During our trip to Scotland, Duncan Hamilton guided us to Loch Lomond for an hour-long cruise on the lake. That day, we had fish and chips for dinner at Margaret and Duncan's house, where they sang old Scottish songs for us. They also guided us on a drive to Ayr to see the beach and enjoy a day of clear blue skies and unseasonably warm weather.

Three months later, Vera was diagnosed with cancer. For the next five months, from October through July, the Hamiltons and Vera spoke weekly over the telephone. Margaret, a cancer survivor herself and a practicing nurse and teacher, advised Vera of the various treatment options and was a sounding board for Vera's questions and fears. Vera came to feel as if Margaret were her sister.

Then we got the surprising and wonderful news that Margaret and Duncan had decided to spend their summer holiday in Arizona with Vera. They both worked three jobs to save for the trip. In fact, they worked seven days a week for six months to make enough for their airline tickets, spending money, and gifts for us. We were excited to see our Scottish friends again, and we secretly hoped and prayed that Vera would survive to see them.

Margaret and Duncan arrived July 1 and remained until July 31. Upon their arrival, they showered us with Scottish gifts. They had purchased a kilt for our three-year-old daughter, Raina; a tartan jumpsuit for our baby, Rory; a hand-knitted doll of a man playing the bagpipes for Vera; a set of Scottish placemats and napkins for me; and so much more. Duncan had driven eighty miles from their house in Scotland to purchase these lovely gifts as tokens of their appreciation for staying in Vera's two-bedroom condominium.

It was not the typical month-long vacation, however. Complete strangers by most definitions, Margaret and Duncan spent hours with Vera in doctors' offices, in hospital waiting rooms, and in pharmacies. They got groceries and prepared nourishing, enjoyable meals for Vera. Margaret, ever the nurse and now a friend, made certain that Vera took her medications properly and even corrected the nurses at the medical center on how to dress Vera's "pic" line for chemotherapy. The Hamiltons even helped with

Vera's most private needs. These amazingly generous people spent their entire holiday month with our family, nursing Vera and giving us all hope.

For most people, a wrong number results in a brief, sometimes even terse, encounter that quickly ends and is quickly forgotten. For some reason, two strangers halfway around the world chose to stay on the line and actually talk to one another. And so a bond was built. Hearts were connected. Lives were intertwined. Was it simply a wrong number? I think not. I choose to believe it was destiny that brought these wonderful wrong-number people into the lives of a special woman and her family in their time of need.

—*Robin Davina Lewis Meyerson*

 Enjoy!

The chocolate-strawberry torte placed before me absolutely dripped decadence, not to mention calories.

"That torte is so rich, it's sinful," I lamented.

Mrs. M., my old friend and person who loves me, was quick to respond. "No, Nancy, the sin would be not to enjoy it."

I laughed. Mrs. M. never lost an opportunity to share her philosophy of life—in a word: *Enjoy!*

She was my mother's age and my grandmother's friend. They met at the millinery shop that Mrs. M. managed and where my grandmother worked as a saleslady. Imagine that: a female manager in the 1940s, when it was virtually unheard of. One reason for her outstanding success was simply that she wore hats well. She could demonstrate the merchandise with style and grace. But she also knew the merchandise and, most important, she knew her customers. That, coupled with her indomitable spirit, gave her the edge.

My first glimpse of her was in the shop window, where she was ingeniously arranging spring creations in anticipation of Easter and Passover. It was admiration at first sight. My grandmother had dressed me up in a new outfit and had taken me to the shop to show me off to the girls. I only had eyes for Mrs. M. She was a regal woman. Tall. Bright and shiny. Classy. Hats that would have looked ridiculous on others rendered her stylish. In my mind, Mrs. M. was a queen.

I remember watching her walk. Her step—quick, confident—sent her short brown curls bouncing. She moved like she knew where she was going and what she was about. One would never guess that she had been born crippled. With strength and determination, she had overcome that handicap.

The disease left her unable to bear children. So, she adopted everyone. My first hint of the depth of her love and compassion for her extended adopted family came when my friend told me that Mrs. M. was paying her tuition at the girls school we attended.

"Why?" I asked. "You aren't even related to her."

"She cares about me," came the simple, yet complete, answer.

Mrs. M. cared deeply about all of the young women

who worked at the shop, "her girls," she called them, and that eventually (and several times) included me.

She gave me my first job when I was thirteen years old, gift-wrapping at Christmastime. As I grew older she tried me in sales, only to find that wasn't my cup of tea, but she didn't give up on me. Instead, she taught me how to do the books, and at sixteen, I was the youngest bookkeeper/cashier ever employed by the millinery. She not only trained me how to keep books, but she also taught me a work ethic that has kept me in good stead all my working life: *Be on time. Be honest. Always try. Do your best. Care about your coworkers and your customers.* It's not that she spouted a litany of catch phrases to me. She taught me by her actions.

When the girls came in before the shop opened, she'd listen as they told her all about their previous evenings and all the happenings in their lives, usually over a cup of coffee. She cared for them like family, and she was interested in them as people.

She treated customers with the same caring and interest. There were many "regulars," some of whom had been coming to the shop for years. They would come in to pay on their layaways, more as an excuse to visit than to make payments. Invariably, someone would ask if she could skip a payment. Mrs. M. always said yes. When a client made the final payment, Mrs. M. brought the hat out with a flourish, positioned it on the new owner's head just so, fussing over the angle of placement and the arrangement of hair beneath. This special attention practically ensured return visits, but that wasn't Mrs. M.'s sole or even most important motivation. It gave her great pleasure to see the confident, satisfied look on a patron's face when she left the store. She knew the value of feeling good about oneself, and she was genuinely pleased to see her customers' faces light up with satisfaction.

During my teen years, when I first worked for her, she became my confidante, the source of much good advice, the ear always willing to listen. She teased me about my boyfriend and made my bridal veil, sewing hundreds of pearls on the tiara. It was no different after my marriage. Three children later, I went back to work for her. When I argued with my husband, she would say, "Life is too short to spend it arguing. Enjoy your husband. Laugh with him."

She practiced what she preached. She traveled extensively with her husband, Frank, enjoying the glitz and glamour of Las Vegas, the horse races and Mardi Gras in New Orleans, and lobster dinners and walks on the beach in Maine. Then, when Frank became blind, she stayed home with him.

It was hard for her to leave the shop, to leave her girls. Some of them were real characters, just like in any family, but she loved them all, quirks and all. To many, she'd been both their boss and mother—and, actually, she didn't see much difference between the roles. Both required discipline and patience. Retiring was a tough choice for Mrs. M. to make, but once she did, she never looked back. At the same time, she also chose to care for her aging and ailing mother.

How she loved them both. Frank, sweet Frank, was the love of her life. She was a small-town girl come to the big city when she met him. He had seen the spark in her and helped stoke it into a lusty flame. He had encouraged and adored her. When the fact was confirmed that she could not bear children, she had been devastated, and he had looked into her eyes and said, "It's you I want, with or without children." During all of their forty-three years of marriage, she was madly in love with him.

When Frank died, God gave her a child to care for: a baby boy, whose mother, the daughter of one of her adopted families, needed a baby-sitter. So began a mutual love affair that persists to this day. Over the years, Mrs. M. has told of his accomplishments and asked for prayers for his struggles. Once, she sent an essay he wrote describing his love of her. A bit tearstained, it came with strict instructions to return it. She prays to the Big Guy Upstairs that she will live long enough to see him graduate from college.

When I moved, Mrs. M. and I began to correspond. I treasure her letters, all of which I've saved, capturing her sage advice. On how to maintain a good marriage she suggests:

Love the hell out of him.
Romance your man; it's fun.
Be lavish with hugs and kisses.
Love him and let him know it.

And, now that I've grown older . . .

Buy some Viagra.

Nearly all of her letters remind me to enjoy life. Be happy. Have fun. Eat good food. Go places. This is the only life you get.

In her advanced years, her body has broken down. She admits to having days when she feels as if nobody loves her, everybody hates her, so she's gonna eat some worms. But they'll be slimy ones, because they'll go down easier.

Sage advice and wonderful letters are not the only things I've received from Mrs. M. Knowing I love to read, she sent me a whole box of paperbacks. When I mentioned that I had decorated my kitchen with strawberries, I suddenly acquired a hand-painted picture of strawberries. When my husband was out of work for an extended period of time and I bemoaned the fact that we couldn't even celebrate our anniversary because of outstanding debts, I received a check and stern directions: "Spend it on dinner and a movie, NOT ON BILLS. Enjoy!"

Though her body may be failing, her mind is not. A great fan of the television show JAG, she claims Commander Harmon "Harm" Rabb "talks" with his eyes. She likes the way he walks. Nash Bridges and Walker don't even come close.

Once she fell and broke two ribs and couldn't breathe. She crawled to the phone and called 911. When asked later where she got the strength to do it, she retorted, "You know you can't keep me down." How true.

Now, Mrs. M. is in her nineties. She is still my mentor, still encourages me in her letters, and still tells me to enjoy life. She makes me laugh with her funny sayings and her descriptions of old age, like the plea I received in a letter. "Send me some dusting powder. I don't want to smell like an old woman."

Mrs. M., with her philosophy of treating each day like a new beginning, reminds me of dawn. She has a freshness about her, a willingness to take risks and to embrace life with all of its hills and valleys, that is like the pure light of the rising sun. I begin every morning with a little ritual. When the sun creeps up and takes its first bow, I whisper, "I'll enjoy this day, Mrs. M."

—Nancy Baker

In My Mother's Heart

Lately, I think about my mother every morning when I hear my daughter leave the house. Rachael likes her space, so I try to stay out of the way while she gets ready for school. I hear the rhythm of her footsteps going up and down the stairs, the water running in the shower, the music in her room, the shutting of drawers and then the door.

Mostly, I hear her leaving. I hear the opening and closing of the noisy garage door, and the sound of the car in reverse as Rachael backs it out of the driveway. I hear her leaving, and I pray for her safety. An hour or so later, I realize that enough time has gone by and no one has called me, and I know she is safe.

I think about my mother at those moments. I now know something about what she went through in those days, when I could not imagine her as I have finally come to know her.

My brother, Kevin, was seventeen, the age Rachael is now, when he left for school one morning and did not return. He was a high school senior, anticipating college and life beyond the family. Now, my daughter is seventeen, with everything ahead of her. Yet, it is a sense, an understanding, of my mother, more than of Rachael or of Kevin, that I feel most strongly these days.

I've been at this place before, as each of my children arrived at this same phase in their life. When my daughter Sara was seventeen, she, like Kevin, was an athlete. A soccer goalie, she had injured her hand in a game. She could not play, she could not write, could not drive. I was acutely aware of the similarities between our lives then and at that other time, some thirty years earlier.

Kevin had broken a knee midway through a basketball game, and true to the athlete he was, he had played the rest of the game. The full-leg cast that followed, though, meant he could not drive his own car to school. So he rode with a friend.

The rain was pouring that February morning. I heard it from my room, where I was trying to stay out of everyone's way and listening to the sounds of our busy house. I heard my mother's voice, disapproving of Kevin's choice of jacket. I heard him leaving. Half an hour later, I heard the radio announce a traffic fatality on Friar's Road. Kevin did not come home again. And all of our lives were changed forever.

As my children were growing up and choosing their own clothes, I rarely argued about what they wanted to wear. I did not always approve, of course, but it did not seem worth a battle. Maybe it had something to do with that morning and that jacket. I have not stopped them from leaving, either, though I know to the core of my being that they might not come back. But I do pray, every morning, all day, and sometimes, it seems, all night long, for their safety out there in the world.

My mother is gone now, but with me in ways I could never have imagined. I now feel more connected to her than ever. She was fifty-six years old when she lost her youngest child, her only boy. I am fifty years old now, and my youngest child is the same age my brother was then. Without the clutter of day-to-day annoyances like the quibbling over a jacket, I see my mother differently now than I did then. I know that she must have felt what I feel. Though I no longer hear her voice, I hear her heart.

—*Therese Madden Rose*

A Hand to Hold

By the time my mother adopted Cory, I was fourteen and accustomed to my mother bringing strangers into the family. There was nothing formal about Mom's adoptions, and the people didn't actually move into our house or relinquish their other family ties. Of all my mother's adoptees, Cory was among the most needy, and she was part of our family the longest. Mostly, I thought of her with irritation and some resentment. But when it really counted, we were there for each other.

Cory was a student in the California school where my mother worked. We were as different as salt from pepper. I was two years older and had topped off before ever reaching five feet tall. Cory was huge—about six feet tall and built like a truck driver, maybe more like a Mack truck. I loved to play piano and to read, sew, and cook; Cory loved all things physical and mechanical.

Cory's father hated that the nearest thing he had to a coveted son was his oldest daughter, Cory. Her mother was afraid of her husband and busied herself with their home and her younger, more feminine daughters. My mother—just barely taller than I am, but with a huge personality and a heart as big as the moon—gave Cory the love and support she missed at home. Cory visited our home often, and she spoke on the phone with my mom for hours.

"She needs me," Mom would say when my sister and I complained that Cory took time that we felt we needed.

Cory became a hippie and lived in one commune after another. Eventually, she settled down a three-hour drive from her then-widowed mother. Then my family relocated to Idaho. The last time I saw her, she had hitchhiked to Idaho to visit my mother. Since I lived nearby, my mother invited me over to visit. We still had nothing in common and little of interest to say to each other. By that time, however, the jealousy was long gone, and we enjoyed a pleasant evening of reminiscing.

During the following years, I got regular "Cory updates" from Mom. In the late 1980s, I was horrified to learn that Cory had been in an industrial accident. She had been working in a gas station, cleaning auto parts, and the owner hadn't provided rubber gloves large enough for her massive hands. With her bare hands, she had dipped the dirty parts into a vat of a clear chemical. She knew immediately that she'd made a serious mistake, but it was too late. The chemical was toxic, and within a few years it had destroyed most of her liver.

My mother went to California and spent days sitting with her in the hospital. Then, Cory's liver seemed to be miraculously on the mend. But her spirits were very low. Three decades had passed since those tenuous teen years, and to me, Cory felt like real family. I was living on the East Coast and had recently lost everything in a disaster. I wanted to do something for Cory, but I, too, was depressed and broke, and couldn't find a way to help. One night I heard a fabulous and very funny storyteller, and I knew: I would send her a couple of the storyteller's tapes to cheer her up.

Cory called me soon after the tapes arrived to tell me how much she'd enjoyed them. We had a wonderful conversation. But with our long history, we knew better than to promise to stay in touch.

Not long after, the lawsuit I'd filed following my disaster finally came to trial—and I lost. I hadn't expected to get all the damages I'd requested, but my lawyer had assured me that my case was strong and that I'd surely get something with which to rebuild my life. I got nothing, zip. I was beaten and broken. Besides the financial loss, I felt abused by the legal system, and my faith in justice and humanity were tattered.

Then Cory called. Just the fact that she'd thought about me and made the effort to pick up the phone and call astounded me. But what really touched me was the love I heard in her voice. For the first time, she exposed the deep, sensitive recesses of her heart. She shared the spiritual lessons she had learned from her own suffering, and she told me that when she was down, she listened to the tapes I'd sent.

"Just the reminder that you cared enough to think of me when you had such troubles of your own makes me feel better," she confided.

As our conversation drew to a close, Cory said, "Growing up, we were never friends. But you never made me feel unwanted, even though I know I was taking a lot of your mom's time. That meant a lot to me then, and it means a lot to me now.

"When you come as close to death as I have, you realize that all that matters is love," she went on. "And Hanna, you're on my love list."

Cory died ten days later of liver failure. During our last conversation, when she reached out and pulled me from the depths of despair, she carved out a special place in my heart. It was a place reserved for family and cushioned with a silken fabric woven from years of caring, which neither of us had noticed until the end.

—*Hanna Bandes Geshelin*

A Solid Investment

"I'd rather use the money to buy a house."

No nine words have ever launched such an emotional debate between my fiancé and me. We may have been two adults sitting at our kitchen table, talking about getting married, but his words took me where I hadn't been in a long time. Suddenly, I was propelled back to grade school, high school, and college—to those times when a young, idealistic girl's dreams help her to escape the drudgery of growing up.

For me, getting married and having a wedding have always meant the same thing. I wasn't prepared to debate a dream I'd had for as long as I'd been brushing my own teeth. It showed.

"If I go to my grave without a wedding, then I go to my grave single." Wow. Even I didn't know I felt so strongly about it. Surely I had grown up enough to separate childish dreams from fundamental needs. Would I really let go of the man I loved based on how we'd spend one day? That's when I started to translate my childhood fantasy into what it meant to me as an adult.

I realized that the day we join our paths forever isn't simply a matter of how we spend that five or six hours. It's not about what we'll wear or eat, where the ceremony will take place, or what song we'll dance to. And the money we spend will be no measure of the day's value.

Any bride over the age of thirty has probably already learned that there is a difference between how she thought life would be and how it actually is. Oddly enough, I now think a wedding is about grown-up realities more than it is about childhood dreams.

After living with David for a year and a half, I know there is no such thing as the perfect man. He gets cranky. His idea of a clean house is worlds apart from mine. He grunts in the morning. But nothing can replace the feeling I get when he calls me at work and we talk about what to make for dinner. I plan to enjoy that comfort forever. It may not always be exciting, but it is real.

And with reality come fights—sometimes, knockdown, drag-out, squint-your-eyes-and-purse-your-lips fights. Both of my sisters and one of my friends are already divorced. As rosy and hope-filled as their weddings were, their experiences have shown me that things can evolve inside a marriage that would awaken any dreamer. I don't need to hear one more divorce statistic to be convinced of how difficult marriage can be.

What I do need is a church full of people to witness our joy as we say our vows. They've certainly been there to witness all the other days of our lives: the day I got braces; the day David took off to trek through Europe; the day I got my first professional job after college. These people have loved, taught, supported, and entertained us. They have molded every memory we have, and helped us to become the people we were when we found each other.

So when I promise to be there in sickness and in health, for richer, for poorer, I want those people to hear me. The day may come when I need a gentle reminder.

I want our wedding to be the celebration to end all celebrations for us. I want to dance with my dad and my stepdad. I want my mom to walk me down the aisle, just as she's walked me through every other step of my life. I want David and me to have that magical day, when our hearts were filled with anticipation and joy, to look back on. I want pictures for our children to look at, to see their parents' love and to help give them dreams of their own.

David has finally given in. We'll get the house someday. For now, I'd rather invest in a foundation—the cement that, from time to time, might be stronger than we are.

—*Julie Clark Robinson*

Six Summers Ago

Six summers ago my mother, my sisters, and I lived on sweet pickles and Granny Smiths. Mom sang to us of the importance of apples, crooning they were food for our brains. To me, then, summertime meant playtime—three glorious months of doing cartwheels in the sun, munching on sweet pickles, and feeding my brain Granny Smiths, oblivious to the changes going on in my body and within myself. Carried weightlessly on the carefree days of my twelfth summer, I never once stopped to look back or forward. Racing toward and crashing through the unyielding forces of adolescence at undeviating speed, I basked in my naive happiness. Looking back now, I sometimes wish I could return, if only for a few moments, to that freewheeling summer of six years ago.

The blazing heat kept us perpetually in our

bathing suits. Although the news (according to Mom) warned to stay out of the sun, that its evil UV rays would char and shrivel us up like bacon, we had our way with the sun. Mom had stockpiled sunscreen and she tried to slather it on my back, as she'd done for eleven summers before—as if I'd still let her. I usually managed to escape her sunscreen attack by mouthing off and showing her that I'd already liberally applied it myself, thank you very much. Then I'd dash to the bathroom and wipe the greasy lotion from my ashen skin and cover myself head to toe with even greasier baby oil. I was determined to get a tan by the first day of seventh grade, even if it meant branding my skin with blisters and pink pillowy scars. Six summers ago, I felt impervious to deadly UV rays and the need for SPF 30, 25, 15, or whatever.

That summer, Mom made a killing from our annual, weeklong garage sale. My sisters and I took turns as cashiers, positioned tall and lanky behind the Nike shoe/cash box. I took pride in my ability to shuffle through tens and twenties, counting out loud and smirking smugly as I dished out change, repeating religiously, "Thank you very much. Have a nice day," while our customers looked on smiling and my sisters took it all in enviously. My sisters, both younger than I am, thought of me as their garage-sale mentor; next summer, maybe, just maybe, they too could deal money like a blackjack dealer.

But the queen bee of our garage sale was Mom. She buzzed in and out of our house every other hour, bringing out piles of old tennis shoes, hangers dripping with worn dresses, and tattered furniture from the basement. Her arms strained as she lugged out chairs, tables, stereos, books, and myriad neglected belongings. I'd turn righteously toward my sisters and wisely advise them, "Go help Mom before she breaks her back." They'd bow their heads obediently and trot off to help, while I expertly made change from a fifty-dollar bill.

By the last Sunday of our sale six summers ago, Mom was running ragged. She had cleared out almost every possible unused and overlooked item from our wardrobes, cupboards, closets, basement, and various nooks and crannies of the house. Then it happened: I can still see with crystal clarity the image of my favorite Barbie—which, although I hadn't played with her in ages and probably never would bother with again, I had always assumed would always be there—being handed over to a bubble gum–chewing girl I was sure would merely toss my doll into her growing heap of garage-sale Barbies. I excused myself from the TV-tray cum cashier-counter, announcing curtly that if my mother wished to sell my cherished Barbies, I wasn't going to be her checkout lady.

My sisters and I then and there decided it was a perfect time to end the garage sale. We reasoned with Mom that it was Sunday, we'd made a good profit, and there was really nothing left to sell. That's when she dove off the deep end. We watched dumbfounded as our mother ripped through the house. We heard her footsteps pound clear through the kitchen, up the stairs, across the carpet, and into her bedroom. As she thundered through her closets, my sisters and I stared holes into the ceiling, fearing she would break through the floor and fall right on us. Five minutes of thumping and bumping later, she hustled down the stairs, nearly missing one of them, clutching to her chest her most treasured childhood memento, her prized piece of American culture, her hunka-hunka burnin love: her beloved velvet Elvis. We braced ourselves for the incredible scene unfolding before us, standing silently before our garage sale–maddened mother as she spoke.

"We have too much stuff in this house. It's time to move on, to make space for bigger and better things," she said as she whisked by us and toward the garage. "If I could sell your Barbie, I can . . ."

She paused, looked my way, and gave me her biggest, warmest, I-understand-just-how-you-feel Mom smile.

"I mean . . . it's just an old picture. Not really worth anything. No big deal. One last sale, that's all, girls."

We nodded robotically. We wouldn't stand in her way. Uh-uh. No way.

"Why are you all looking at me like I'm a crazy person? Keep moving on to bigger and better things. Remember that, girls."

Yeah, Mom, but Elvis is the king of rock and roll. Elvis is your hero.

Six summers ago, my dad delighted the family with a swimming pool, a used aboveground job he bought from a guy across town. Daddy laid the foundation, poured the gravel, bought a solar cover, and invested in mass amounts of chlorine. We smothered him with hugs and thank-yous for his gift of a swimming pool in our own backyard "for his girls," which, of course, included Mom.

While Dad worked his butt off Monday through Friday, my sisters and I bathed in the holy water of our pool. Mom made us her special iced tea, the only kind worth drinking, her secret ingredient hidden deep inside her sacred, gingham-clad recipe book. The deck of the pool served as our sleeping bay, reading nook, and a stage reserved for the talented few who were daring enough to belt out Boyz II Men songs to our adoring audience: Mom, who rewarded our off-key renditions with an exuberant round of applause and a standing ovation.

In mid-August, the meteorologists gave the go-ahead to go out in the sun, as long as you wore SPF 30. Mom began to dangle the remainder of summer in our faces, preaching of its impending end.

"Enjoy it while you can, girls. Summer is almost o-v-e-r."

By then we had turned our attentions to school clothes and daytime soap operas, having filled up on the sun, pool escapades, sweet pickles, and Granny Smiths during June and July. Meanwhile, I'd taken to heart the beauty advice in my teenybopper magazine and, following the latest tress trend of the season, had my mom chop off my hair. I'd also outgrown Kmart and discovered the mystique of the mall. I couldn't understand why Mom didn't understand that acid-washed jeans weren't cool anymore. I was ready for seventh grade, ready to play soccer, ready to go to concerts with my girlfriends, and ready to kiss a boy.

Oh, once in a while during the lazy last days of that summer six years ago, I'd venture outside, squinting my eyes to keep the shards of sunlight from piercing my eyes as I peered at the grapes to see if they'd ripened yet. At least, that's what I told my mom. Actually, I was peeking at a new boy with a nice smile and a great laugh who tied vines in the fields behind my house. My teenybopper magazine had told me to go for him, to make the first move, that guys were into aggressive girls then, six summers ago. In the month it took me to get up the nerve and figure out a way to approach him, he'd finished tying all the grapes and was gone, leaving me with my unsung preteen rhapsody.

Though the yellow sun crept up our backs, chasing the fall chill from the air, I was convinced my summer was over. I'd already left it and my childhood behind, and was poised to burst through the autumn leaves as an adult. Hadn't Mom said to move on to bigger and better things? Hadn't she sold her velvet Elvis so she could move on? Hadn't I sold my childhood to summer, starting with my favorite Barbie, so I could move on?

Six summers later, I reflect on all the bigger and better ways in which my sisters and I and even our parents have moved on. I now realize there is no such thing as "bigger and better." Who we are and what we have are good enough, often better than we realize, just as they were then, six summers ago, just as they are now and at any given moment in our lives.

Six summers ago, in my twelve-year-old innocence, I didn't question myself or the world around me. It was just another summer, and I readily accepted its gifts of sweet pickles and Granny Smiths, Mom's iced tea, and Dad's swimming pool. I never once considered how he hard he'd worked to buy it and install it himself, so that his girls could have a wet haven to cool them in the summer sun. As summer came to an end, I hurled myself toward adulthood, intent on growing up, unaware the process had already begun with the manning of the TV stand at the garage sale. Only later, only recently, did I realize that on that last Sunday of our garage sale six summers ago, my mom sold her velvet Elvis not to move on to bigger and better things, but to cool the sting of her daughter's growing pains after selling her favorite Barbie.

Six summers ago, the sun singed my shoulders pink, but no sunburn scars mark the transition to bigger and better things during that last summer of my childhood. All that remains are memories of the biggest and best thing of all . . . love.

—Heidi Kurpiela

Tree of Life

I don't know when I fell in love with trees and with climbing them. I think perhaps I was born with this urge, just as my father before me and my son after me.

While growing up, my cousin Wanda and I spent many long, lazy summer weeks together at her family cottage in Grand Marais, Minnesota. The cottage itself was very basic—built of cardboard and wood; dated, mismatched furniture and linens; basin and well for washing; outhouse at the far back corner of the lot. It had several sets of bunk beds where we slept only when we absolutely had to.

The magic of the place was to be found beyond the walls of the cottage—at the beach. I loved the water, the waves, the sand, and the sun, but mostly, I loved the trees. Nestled behind the sand dunes, in a secret world that tickled the imagination of my nine-year-old self, was my tree, Christopher. Wanda had her own tree, which we were certain was the biological sibling to my tree. Her tree became Christine. Just as the brother tree and the sister tree grew side by side—their branches intermingled, yet their trunks unique—so did Wanda and I grow like siblings. We were moved by the winds of similar pleasures and came to know each other's differences, yet we felt the comfort of being rooted in our love for each other.

We spent hours lost in our tree world. I don't remember ever having to share my tree with anyone. I came to believe that if trees can belong to a person, then Christopher belonged to me. My muscles memorized the exact placement of his branches, and my skin knew the many knots of his trunk. Within thirty seconds I could climb to my favorite spot, as tender branches glanced my skin, like strokes from a good friend. Perched there, halfway up Christopher's full height, I felt as if I had become one with the tree and all the life that dwelt there. Like a sparrow, camouflaged amongst the leaves, I had a bird's-eye view of the sloping dunes in all directions, and I felt freer and more alive than when my feet were on the ground.

A few years later, another tree entered my life when my fifth-grade class went on a field trip to the Sandilands Forest. We were each given a seedling to take home. I remember rummaging through the

garage to find a shovel, digging a hole in the backyard, and gently lowering the root of the prickly
green strand into the soil. I christened the baby evergreen with water, tenderness, and the name Christopher. My child mind couldn't seem to get enough of
that name.

Many years later I would forget about both of my
Christopher trees. I was other-focused as my husband,
John, and I prepared for our shift into parenthood.
Our first child came into the world by cesarean section. While I was still numb from mid-sternum down,
my mouth and throat like dry sand, they showed me
my newborn son. His eyes were squinty, and the top
of his skull was flattened, making his head look like a
chubby triangle of flesh on bones. I was stunned that
this fully formed human had come from my body. His
frail, imperfect beauty intoxicated me.

The babe was whisked away to the nursery while
the doctors stitched me up. My husband instinctively
followed the baby, leaving me to my numbness and
thoughts. I searched my mind for a fitting name for
our baby boy. Who did he look like? Not really an
Andrew or a Carl, the names we'd placed at the top
of our negotiated list. A name came to me. It was
somewhere near the bottom of our agreed-upon
favorites, but it suddenly seemed just right.

Meanwhile, in the nursery, John watched and
crooned as the baby was sponged, weighed, measured,

and bundled. He began to call the child by name, almost without hesitation. Soon after, when the three of us were all reunited in my room, he nervously approached me.

"I know we haven't decided the name yet," he said, "but I have to tell you . . . I started calling him Christopher." At that moment I knew our souls had communicated: John's, mine, Christopher's, and the Great Spirit, for that was the name I had felt, too.

A few days later I received a visit from my cousin Wanda. She came into the hospital room smiling and saying, "I can't believe you named your son after a tree."

In that instant, it all came back to me. How could I have forgotten those glorious days with Wanda and Christopher and Christine? The universe had spoken. And so it is that my soul-mate son shares his name with two other soul mates in my life: Christopher the Poplar and Christopher the Spruce.

—*Hedy Wiktorowicz Heppenstall*

Technicolor Dreams

I have always dreamed in Technicolor. Rather than the ordinary shadowed, murky dreams or the blinding-light dreams, mine are vivid, full-on explosions of color.

I wonder whether it is in the genes?

My great-grandmother, Bongie, too, had grand Girl-Go-West dreams, which took her from Paoli, Indiana, to the flat grassy plains of Kansas, where her parents put down roots. Their wagons carried dreams and hopes, and the tools to make them real, while far away a blue-and-gray war raged, spilling red upon field and stone.

Did Bongie see color in her dreams?

I have a picture of Bongie and my great-grandfather sitting in front of their homestead shack in Caldwell, Idaho. Behind them, the wide sepia sky and the dry brown earth seem to stretch on forever. They are passing their Sabbath reading the newspaper and doing handiwork. Bongie wears spectacles on her nose and thick gray hair piled atop her head. She had come far from Paoli, this teacher of Kiowa and ex-slave children, mother of four, spinner of flax and stories. A proper Victorian who had seen Abe Lincoln before he left his home state to become president, she put her foot down when one of her daughters wanted to go to "gay Paree" to live along the Seine and paint colorful impressions, but stood by that same daughter when she took her Brownie camera, recorded the Cheyenne and Comanche in black and white, and brought them to life in the darkroom.

Some dreams get altered, but the colors remain true.

My Nana, another of Bongie's girls, had dreams of home, of finding her Puritan ancestors in New England. After going to business school, she married and followed the railroad with her accountant husband across the West—Oklahoma, New Mexico, Idaho—before they were states. She saw it all: cow towns, mining towns, little towns on the edge of nowhere.

As my grandfather advanced his career, she sewed her own clothes, played her Spanish guitar, and added sons until she had three. Once, she settled down long enough for her boys to play football for a deaf school, the only hearing players on the team. They would listen for the other teams' plays, and then pass them on to their teammates in sign language. They always won. In World War I, they were doughboys. Then, at forty, Nana birthed my mother and settled down in Boise, Idaho, for the next fifty-nine years.

I loved my nana, loved the soft velvety feel of her cheek against mine. Loved the sound of her voice, soft with its Western lilt. "I went fer a walk up the crik," she'd say, or, "None of your beeswax."

She had dreamed of my mother. Did she dream of me?

On my bedroom mirror I have a black-and-white photograph of my mother. She is sitting on a rail fence at her uncle's ranch north of Boise, where she herded turkeys one summer on horseback. The rolling grass hills in the background are dry and nearly treeless. She wears logger's boots laced up to her knees and a floppy hat. She is looking at the camera and smiling—a warm and inviting smile, the smile that has been my lifelong balm to hurts and worries. In the picture, she is a young woman with rich auburn hair, and beautiful.

Maybe she was thinking of going up to the hot springs and plunging into the steamy, thick waters to get the dust off. Or maybe she was thinking about the CCC boys in the camp up the creek. Their reveille wakes everyone up early, and their Easternness is foreign when they come down into her aunt's country store. One of them wants to be a musician, but times are hard.

My mother had dreams—piano-keyed, Schubert-Chopin dreams that took her from the hot, dry gulches of southwestern Idaho to the lush green campus of the University of Michigan in Ann Arbor, where she studied with the best. She wore the clothes my nana made, as fine as any tailor's, and met my scientist father over cookies at the dorm.

Her musique-conservatoire-in-Switzerland dreams and concerts-on-the-Seine dreams were cut short by World War II. And then they were sidetracked by life in hot, humid Washington, D.C., as my brothers and I ran riot on the stairs.

But still she held to her dreams, and the colors ran true.

I have a wonderful memory. We've moved to Pittsburgh. I'm lying in my bed. The door is closed, and the room is dark, but through the door comes the sound of my mother's Baldwin piano downstairs. A violin and cello are accompanying her. The other musicians are scientists, and they are playing

Schubert's "Trout Quintet." I am very young. I think of fish and deep pools of color, as the rich sounds of the music eddy and flow.

The music will sustain me all of my life. The music will become words. And forty years later, my mother will see her dream come true at music workshops in Salzburg, in Oxford, and in the mountains of Tyrol.

Another memory comes to me. I am four years old and looking dreamily into a fishbowl. My nose is on its edge, and my hair is as light and wispy as corn silk. So young, I don't yet see the direction I should go with my life, don't yet see my dream. There will be false starts and dead ends.

Then, at sixteen, I'll take my nana's Spanish guitar and sing my way to an "A" in French class. I'll spin flax and go to France and walk along the Seine in gay Paree. I'll write folk songs and meet the man of my dreams on the sands of Waikiki. I'll have three sons. And I will live in the West.

Now, I have dreams of writer-gets-published, and of teaching history so compellingly that a child says, "Cool!"

These dreams that I dream in vivid, full-on Technicolor are the dreams of my grandmothers and mother. They are all one. And the colors run true.

—Janet Oakley

Laura: Moving Friends Forever

Walking in the crisp morning air, I feel once again the power of love. It is Sunday morning, our time, my friend-for-life and me. We have both been out of town, so it has been weeks since we've walked. We are religious about this ritual; we count on it, like breathing and afternoon naps. We have lots to talk about, stories to tell, adventures to share. But it is not really the words that matter, it is just being together, and moving. We know what we have is precious, and we are demonstrative, as always, in our greeting. We cling briefly to each other and then off we go.

We have been striding side by side together for more than twenty years, through all kinds of weather and family turmoil. Laura discovered me one day, as I was coming home from a run, and anointed me her new running partner. I confessed straight out to being a fair-weather short-distance runner, despite my well-developed calves, which is what had attracted her in the first place. She was unfazed and said she would have my distance up in no time. Who was this woman so determined to get me out on the road? As it turns out, she was right. Pretty soon, in spite of myself, we were doing five miles three times a week. I had always hated running and only did it so that I could eat what I wanted and stay fit. With Laura, I forgot I was running. We talked the whole time, holding nothing back. We laughed out loud. And we became friends.

I doubt that we gave our running routine or our friendship much thought in those early years. We were too busy worrying over our young children, wondering if they would be toilet-trained by kinder-garten, and complaining about our husbands, those insensitive men too caught up in their own lives to pay close attention to ours.

We were older first-time parents, in our early thirties with our cesarean-born baby boys. We took for granted our youth and good health.

Years passed. Laura had a second baby boy, and shortly thereafter, so did I. We were mothers of sons; we had a lot in common. We kept running—and talking—trusting each other with our deepest secrets. Fueled by adrenaline, we held nothing back and opened ourselves to each other's advice. There was plenty, and it always helped, at least for my part. We ran through an almost-affair or two, occasional marital discord, work changes, and childhood traumas. We ran through damp dark evenings and hot sunny afternoons, changing clothes to fit the seasons, adjusting days and times to fit our schedules, but always, always running and talking.

Laura is my moving friend. We took up biking for a while when she had an injury that prevented running. A few times, we risked death as we misjudged oncoming traffic and slick rain-drenched roads. Biking impeded our conversation some, but it was only a temporary adjustment. We were nothing if not adaptable.

Soon we were back to our old running pattern. Once we were so engrossed in conversation that we didn't hear a man coming up from behind. It was dark and windy, and we were leaning close together, oblivious to the world around us. When we heard the heavy breathing right next to us, we screamed and grabbed each other, and scared the heck out of that poor runner, who'd had the temerity to blurt out "runner on the left" and pull us out of our reverie. After he passed, trembling in his own fear, we laughed uproariously at the power of our screams. We were invincible. We could handle anything.

Then I took up soccer and began an exhilarating four-year process of wrecking my body. Eventually, I had to quit running distances. We tried having tea together, but it didn't work. Laura could not—would not—sit still. I thought that was the end of us. Instead, we decided to try walking, and so began our Sunday dates.

We found a route that satisfied us both, with enough hills to challenge and very little traffic to cause distraction. We continued to move and talk fast, rushing downhill toward the waterfront, cruising along the flats, and puffing back up the other side. We continued to share the trials, tribulations, and intermittent joys of parenthood in our hurried, breathy fashion. We sandwiched in those walks, just like the runs before them, between the real tasks of life: our jobs and families mostly.

We had our small adventures, including the time we saw a naked man doing his own brand of yoga overlooking Puget Sound. And the day we passed a man jogging toward us who was so gorgeous that we had to turn around and stare at his retreating butt—only to discover that his butt was bare under his long running shirt. We were thrilled and searched him out for weeks afterward, hoping to catch another glimpse and eventually wondering if we had made him up.

Then I got cancer, and everything changed. At first I refused to see Laura, because I didn't think I could handle her reaction. She is a woman of intense emotion—we are alike in that way—and I knew this turn of events had slammed her hard. Years before, she had been more upset than I was by my early miscarriage. Also, her mother had died of cancer, and she had her own personal scars from this disease. So, I kept her at a distance until she promised not to come unglued. She came over to see me, which was so weird, the two of us just sitting in my living room trying to act casual about the tumor that had grown between us. When I couldn't stand her pained smile any longer, I relented in exasperation, "Oh, hell, let it go!" She did, and we cried, and laughed, and then cried some more, all that pent-up emotion demanding release.

And then we did what we knew how to do best. We moved. We kept walking, through months of chemo and radiation. I couldn't manage the hills anymore, so every Sunday I drove us down to the waterfront so that we could walk the flats. We struck out, arm-in-arm, resolute and scared. She always made sure my bald head was bundled against the winter cold. I teased her about that, but I liked the way she looked after me. She told me that someday we'd look back on this time as a mere blip in the greater scheme of things. I said that, no, this thing was big, and we would never be the same. She nodded reluctantly and withdrew her naive words of reassurance. Sometimes we passed friends who said how good I looked, sometimes strangers who said they were praying for me. It had its surreal moments.

Those walks became sacred—our Sunday school, in a way—and something I was determined to do no matter what, pretty much. We walked more slowly, because my feet had gone flat and lifeless due to the vincristine in my chemo cocktail, and also because my energy was as low as a tadpole in wintertime. We laughed more and cried some. We held hands and hugged when we needed to, and we didn't give a rat's behind what anybody thought about any of it. All those years of worrying about our kids, complaining about our husbands, grieving the deaths of parents, and adjusting to Laura's new stepmom—none of it had prepared us for the possibility of losing each other.

Now that I am healthy again, we have picked up the pace. We cruise up and down those long hills, rain or shine. We take nothing for granted. We have come to know, in a way that is as intense as a rainbow over Puget Sound, that we are blessed. I amble over to her house, and we discuss how cold or hot it is outside. We adjust our clothes accordingly, adding gloves or discarding jackets. We hug and giggle and head down the hill, blowing off steam about the events of the week. I stop to yell at a couple of crows, and we laugh at my outlandishness. As we hit the flats along the waterfront, at about mile two, we move into full swing. We see a seal cavorting in the waves, and we actually pause for a moment to appreciate the sight. We *ooh* and *ahh* at the light reflecting off the seal's back, and we hold onto each other in joyful abandon.

We are each other's best audience, and we know it. We are in church, and it is a holy place, and we are paying attention. We realize how fragile it all is, in a way we could not have fathomed in those early days. Maybe because of that, we are sassier than ever, walking through the seasons, worrying about our kids, complaining about our husbands, and celebrating our ability to do so. We are more philosophical these days about most things, perhaps because we went to the brink of the abyss, and we saw what it looked like over the edge.

Laura and I love each other in a way that only best girlfriends can, unconditionally and with an honesty rarely shared in other relationships. I know that she will always be there for me, and I trust that she knows that I will always be there for her. She is my moving friend, and we are at our best when we're charging uphill, deeply engaged in matters of great importance—at least to us. As we walk and talk, laugh and rant, we are steady and true to our path and, most especially, to one another.

—*Janie H. Starr*

The Women Who Made Me

I was born lucky. I am the creation of several women. Though only my mother holds the honor of literally birthing and raising me, three other female family members had a hand in my making, just as surely as if they had molded me of clay. These women—my mother, two of my paternal aunts, and one unofficial aunt—were once bigger than life to me and even now that I recognize them as all too human, they still loom large in my life. They all had impact, each in her unique way. Their potpourri of personalities determined, to a significant extent, the girl I was and the woman I am.

From my mother came the contribution of heart. She passed on to me her generosity and kindness. Her softness smoothed my hard edges. She infused me with her love of people and conversation and the genuine joy of gift giving. To my mother also goes the credit for my aversion to being a housewife, her chosen role in life. I saw her faith trampled when her marriage to my father ended and she had little else to sustain her. I looked at my mother and her life, and I made a 180-degree about-face and headed the opposite way, vowing never to be the dependent one.

My aunts from my father's side were my role models for adult life. I fashioned myself after them without even realizing it. I am of my mother, but so like my aunts. Aunt Lee was the fireball in our family. Short, feisty, and defiant, she was always in charge and let you know it. She was never without an opinion and never hesitated to express it. If Aunt Lee knew what was best for you, she would tell you—whether you wanted to hear it or not. People listened to Lee, whom I affectionately referred to as the "Gestapo."

As infuriating as the little Gestapo has sometimes been, Aunt Lee has also been a treasure. She gave me her strength, her energy, her hard work, and her conviction. She taught me that opinions are good things to have and that I was entitled to mine. From Aunt Lee, I received the right to say what I think and the confidence to go out and get what I want. By her example, I learned the value of being in charge, especially of your own life.

Aunt Anna, one of my older aunts, was a strong yet subtle influence. She was an interesting combination of silence and iron will. Aunt Anna was the rock of the family, and many people, including me for many years, thought she was cold. Then one day I saw Aunt Anna break down. Her lapse of control lasted only a moment. She was discussing my father, her favorite brother, who had just died. When she spoke, her voice cracked, but she willed herself to continue speaking and regained control. By the sheer force of her will, she stopped her emotions in their tracks. That day, I realized the extent of Aunt Anna's willpower and the depth of her character. In a split second, I saw beyond the stern exterior and learned more about Aunt Anna than I had from years of observation. I am still amazed by her ability to rein in her tears.

From Aunt Anna, I received the gifts of dignity, pride, and self-containment. I learned that I could make a statement without speaking. She taught me that some feelings are private, and wearing them on your sleeve minimizes them. I realized that Aunt Anna's reserve was a form of self-preservation, a way of holding on to herself to keep from breaking apart. For me, that was a hard lesson to learn, but eventually I learned when and how to emulate her strength and self-control.

My one unofficial female family influence, who has never been awarded the title of "aunt," was Joan. She was a woman ahead of her time. Joan lived with my favorite uncle, Charlie, who was still someone else's husband. For this unforgivable infraction, Joan's family had disowned her. Though she was younger than my parents and their siblings, because of her relationship with my uncle, Joan was part of their generation. But Joan stood out. She was the only older person in my family whom I considered a friend, not just a relative.

I now know that I was drawn to Joan because she did what she wanted and took herself to wherever she wanted to go. In a family of women who did not drive, that was big stuff. From Joan I learned the joyful liberation of as well as the loneliness of independence. Years later, I realized the fierce price she had paid for her liberty. Eventually, I think it broke her heart.

Joan taught me that flirting was fun and men were not some strange, mysterious enemies. She showed me that you could have fun with the guys and still act like a lady. Joan taught me to look for the few good men who would treat me as an equal and yet want and appreciate me as a woman. I can still see Joan, with her short, dark hair, head thrown back in laughter, having the time of her life. She loved every meal she ever ate. She grabbed life by the shirt collar and shook it. She did things that no one else in our family would even think of doing. The first time I flew in an airplane I was with Joan.

These are the women who made me. I am the

combined creation of their spirits and my own. Their strengths and quirks are now entwined with mine. I carry their imprints forward, as I make my own.

—*Donna Marganella*

Kneading the Bonds of Friendship

I love visiting Anna's house. It's full of calm kindness and positive energy. Some people have the knack of creating good space. It's the knack of keeping hands and minds busy. It's the knack of paying attention. It's also the knack of being a good friend and passing wisdom along, even while making bread. Anna has it.

One morning, Anna called me. "I'm going to make cinnamon bread. I know you like cinnamon bread and I know you want to watch the bread machine, so I won't start it until you're here."

On my last visit, nearly a month ago, Anna served hot rye bread from her new bread machine. The machine was a thoughtful Christmas present from her daughter. I asked whether sometime I could be there while she made bread.

I arrive to find bread-making ingredients ready and chili simmering for lunch. Anna offers fresh, hot coffee. I love it when other people cook. To me, it's magic to pour lots of stuff into pitcher or pot and have it come out when and what it's supposed to be. Maybe it's the magic of knowing and using the talents we each have. Maybe, if I watch long enough, a little of this cooking talent will rub off on me.

Anna starts the bread. Everything gets poured into a sort of bucket. It doesn't look like a loaf pan. "That can't come out as bread," I say.

Anna laughs. "You'll see."

The bucket goes into the machine and Anna pushes some buttons. Soon, there are ghastly mixing and kneading noises.

"Shouldn't you go check?"

"It's fine. We'll have lunch and hot bread later for dessert."

The chili is just spicy enough. Its green peppers are from Anna's brother's garden. The bread machine occasionally moans and clanks and then stops to think about things. We have second bowls of chili, and I keep waiting for the machine lid to fly off or something else to make terrible noises.

Anna rinses the dishes and puts a bowl of chili aside for her brother. The bread machine is now suspiciously silent.

"Are you sure you shouldn't go check it?"

"The bread has to rise more than once, and then it will bake. We'll go in the living room."

Anna picks up the afghan she is crocheting. These days, she uses light-colored yarn because she can see it better.

"I gave up a lot when I had to stop driving," she says, "but I still find things to do."

We talk about her friends and neighbors, many of whom she's kept in touch with for fifty years. She mentions the weekly phone conversation with her daughter. She tells me that her granddaughter likes the double-bed afghan she finished for her last month. The whole family will come, as usual, for Thanksgiving.

She's glad grass-mowing is over for this year and wonders whether she will be able to do it next summer. She talks about her plans to get the downstairs rooms painted. She asks about my new computer and about my brother, who has not been well.

I tell her what I've been up to, but I keep half an ear out for the machine in the kitchen. I don't hear anything. I can't smell any baking going on either.

Anna crochets, unconcerned. I wonder how much of her time has been measured in skeins of yarn passed through her hands to be passed in time to someone else. This afghan is for a nephew. "He likes to watch TV on the floor, and it will be cold soon. After this, the church bazaar wants one."

I have one of Anna's afghans, one that she made right after she was diagnosed with macular degeneration, which affects the retina. It was one of many "experiments" as she learned to do things in new ways. Magnifiers, tape recorders, and Hi-marks (to label appliance and thermostat dials) have become part of her life. I often wrap myself in her determination on winter nights.

We stretch and climb her steep steps to the only bathroom. These steps help keep her legs and lungs working. I sniff. (After all, warm air rises.) She laughs.

"You have to have more faith."

"It's been more than an hour since we've even been in the kitchen."

We come back downstairs. She laments that long walks are getting tougher, though she still makes herself walk whenever the weather allows. She goes to the kitchen for water and her blood-pressure medication. I follow, wanting to get closer to you-know-what.

And suddenly, I smell baking bread. "Something's happening."

Anna walks to the machine to check the timer. "It won't be long now."

And soon, the machine beeps; the bread is finished. And it is real bread. It makes the whole downstairs smell cozy. It tastes like it was worth all that waiting.

Anna slices a second piece for me before I can ask.

"I put a little extra cinnamon in it. I know you like cinnamon."

—Nancy Scott

Steering into Safe Waters

When I was eighteen, I was accepted to a college that proceeded to declare bankruptcy the summer following my high school graduation, just weeks before I was to leave home and find my way. Faced with no other plans, I climbed into a friend's tightly packed car, and the two of us headed off to San Francisco. After a week of sleeping on the floor of a relative's condo, I signed a lease for a third-floor flat on the corner of Cole and Haight, home of sleeping drunks and sleepless teenagers. I had vague thoughts of being the next Virginia Woolf or Emily Dickinson, so I took the streetcar and a bus to San Francisco State University and enrolled. I had arrived in San Francisco with about a thousand dollars. After paying for the flat and tuition, I had enough left over for several boxes of macaroni and cheese. It was time, I realized, to face the empty fridge, get a job, and grow up.

Seventeen years later, I had a fairly useless degree in English along with a full-time job in admissions, two lovely children, and not much else. I had certainly grown up, and had left behind my charming alcoholic husband—and all dreams of a room of my own. My creative writing degree was put to waste writing procedural manuals and meeting minutes, but I couldn't grouse too much. After all, I was paying my way after being left broke and fending off creditors. Alone and with my university job, at least I had health benefits, a house, and peace of mind, and my children wore decent clothes to school. Though I wasn't Emily Dickinson, I wasn't living in a Dickens novel either.

I usually arrived at the office by 7:00 in the morning so I could be out of there by 4:00 in the afternoon. I liked getting off work early enough to pick up the kids at day care and treat them to pizza or a rented video. My friends teased me about my romantic Friday nights. But after years of wondering what Friday nights with my drunken husband might bring, the security I felt with just my two kids in tow and nothing more unpredictable than what flavor ice cream they might buy was excitement enough for me.

Along the way I've met other women like me— women who seem adrift at first but then steer the course of their lives like steadfast sailors through a storm, arriving in calm waters and happy to be there. One of these women, my dear friend Katie, has had a particularly strong impact on my life.

Katie had barely finished high school before she became the mother of two kids, before she could even think about what she might do with her life. Then came several years of living in the suburbs, private school for the kids, holidays and vacations celebrated with lots of food, and lots and lots of drinking. She had a third child, and five years later, another one. As her husband focused on his work, Katie focused on raising their children, on cooking and cleaning up after a family of six, trying always to keep everyone in good order and in good humor. Her husband continually drank more, talked less, and smoldered in anger, while Katie threw herself into being superwoman and into her own drinking. But it's hard to steer the course when you're floating on alcohol. Katie felt trapped in a large house caring for a large family, with years of family history to keep her tethered to the mast of their lives together. Then, one day, she took the helm.

Someone had told her about Alcoholics Anonymous. She attended meetings, and something began to move in her heart. She joined an outpatient program and stopped drinking. She signed up for vocational counseling and rediscovered her longing to be a nurse (maternity, of course). While one daughter started college and another started kindergarten, Katie started her first basic classes.

Katie continues to learn how to use the currents to move in new directions and, ultimately, in the right direction. In so doing, she is charting new territory for herself and her family. Her family often complains, of course, and sometimes they even try to get things back on the old track. After all, the familiar often seems the better choice, initially. But Katie saw something golden on the horizon and, like me, she set sail for that distant shore, and she just holds tight and keeps her focus when the water gets choppy. She knows the struggle is well worth it, when the waters are calm and everything feels safe, yet a new adventure is just ahead.

Sometimes on Fridays, Katie and I steer our ships toward each other. We grab our kids, and we all go out together for dinner. Afterward, we take them to the park to play, while Katie and I sit quietly together, talking, laughing, and dreaming.

—*Sarah Stockton*

Two American Ladies

I was almost fourteen when I boarded the old Navy ship, *The General M. B. Stewart*, in the port of Bremen, Germany. I was with my grandparents and hundreds of other people, many of them Hungarians like us, who were fortunate enough to have survived the refugee camps. World War II had torn apart our lives and displaced us, making us refugees. Though our arms ached from all the required shots, our hopes and dreams soared as we began our journey to America.

Once aboard ship, women and children were ushered to one huge area below deck, men and older boys to another. Then we were all assigned sleeping quarters. I got the upper bunk, Grandma the lower. Grandpa, of course, went with the men. After settling in with our meager belongings, a few items of clothing, Grandma and I joined Grandpa up on deck, where we knew he was waiting for us.

As the ship pulled out to sea, the people on shore shouted *"Auf Wiedersehen"* (until we meet again), and many on board had tears in their eyes, for we knew we would never see our homeland again. I remember studying my grandparents' faces; their teary eyes revealed the bittersweet feeling I shared. But we were on our way to America now, where the streets were paved with gold! Well, maybe not actual gold, Grandpa had explained, but with golden opportunities.

We had heard so much about America from friends and relatives who had gone before us. Two years before our departure, I started studying English in the refugee camp school, but my command of it was still poor.

Our Atlantic crossing took ten days, most in raging, stormy seas. My grandmother was seasick much of that time, but I thrived and soon made some new friends. A young American named Dave, who worked in the enormous galley, brought me my first Coke, a new taste delight. Then he asked me where I was going in America.

"I go to India," I had told Dave, shyly.

He smiled at me and said, "That's probably Indiana, not India. In-di-an-a," he emphasized the last part, adding, "You will like America."

"In America, everything will be okey-dokey." I

giggled, using the new phrase I had picked up from Dave.

Most of the kids on the ship whiled away the hours playing games and watching Roy Rogers movies in the huge recreation room. There was also plenty of excitement. One day while a friend and I were sharing an easy chair, an enormous wave hit the ship, throwing the chair across the room, sending us and everyone else in its path scrambling for safety. In the enormous mess hall, where we took all our meals, we often had to hold on to our trays with one hand as we ate to keep them from sliding off the table. Topside, we'd often watch dolphins at play in the water, bobbing up and down in the great waves. Sometimes, we even saw other ships passing, like the luxury ship *The Queen Elizabeth,* heading toward Europe with its American passengers! When we chugged past the White Cliffs of Dover, we sang "There'll Be Blue Birds over the White Cliffs of Dover," which someone in the recreation room had taught us.

Then, one morning before dawn, my grand-mother awakened me. "Hurry, get up, sweetheart. The lights of New York are visible in the distance!" she told me excitedly. I jumped down from my bunk and dressed quickly, and then we headed out to the deck, where hundreds of people had already gath-ered. Grandfather was there, waiting for us. I remember gazing sleepily into the black distance, becoming slowly entranced by the trillions of lights out there on the dark horizon. It looked like a fairy-land. It was my first look at America!

Just as dawn broke, someone in the crowd shouted, "There she is! There she is! The Statue of Liberty!"

Mesmerized, I gazed upon the vision of that grand lady with the torch rising magnificently out of the sea. From my vantage point on the ship, she seemed to hold her torch higher and higher on the New York skyline. I was overcome with emotion and could almost hear Lady Liberty saying the words I had learned in English class: "Give me your tired, your poor, your huddled masses yearning to breathe free." And it seemed she was speaking directly to me. That vision is indelibly etched in my memory.

Later, as we pulled into the harbor, the "Star-Spangled Banner" played over the loudspeakers, and we learned that it was the national anthem of our new country. Once again, tears filled the eyes of those on board.

We had arrived in America!

After several hours of being processed on Ellis Island, my grandparents and I were finally released to our sponsor's wife, Mrs. Levin. We traveled with her by train to our new destination, Indiana. During the long train ride, I answered her questions in my broken English, painfully aware of my shabby condition. I thought she was the most beautiful, kindest woman I had ever met.

Mrs. Levin helped us get settled into the small house they had ready for us. A few days later, she stopped by with some news for me.

"You will be going to school soon, so tomorrow you and I are going shopping," she said with a bright smile. "How old did you say you are?"

"In two months I will be fourteen," I replied.

"Well, I was thinking that a young lady of almost fourteen might like to get rid of her little-girl braids, so we'll visit a beauty shop tomorrow, too." Her smile was so kind and bright that I had the urge to hug her.

The following day, a transformation began under Mrs. Levin's kind guidance. I got a stylish new haircut and stylish American clothes and shoes. Then she took me to see my first movie, *Father of the Bride*, where I got a further boost to my adolescent self-confidence when a couple of teenaged boys "made goo-goo eyes" at me in the lobby. At least that's what Mrs. Levin said they were doing. She shared many other insights and in many other ways helped this shy young Hungarian girl blossom into a self-confident young American woman.

So it was, that on a bright September day in 1951, I met two special American ladies who forever changed my life: one who welcomed me into the land of promise, and one who helped show me the promise within me and how to make my way in this golden land. I will always remember Mrs. Levin's kindness and Miss Liberty's warm welcome.

—*Renie Szilak Burghardt*

A Little Taste of Heaven

I t was late at night. The sheriff had just left, and my husband and I were trying to deal with our worst nightmare. Our son, Mike, who had conquered his quadriplegia by transforming himself into a wheelchair athlete, had died. I tried to pull myself together to make the necessary phone calls. I was strangling, the lump in my throat making it nearly impossible to speak.

I dialed my friend Elaine, who had loved Mike nearly as much as we did. When I said the awful words, she didn't dissolve into tears or even ask what had happened. Her first words to me were, "What can I do?"

It wasn't the first time I'd turned to her in a crisis. Years earlier I had called to tell her about an unexpected pregnancy in the family. "How wonderful!" she said, jolting me out of my despair. In an instant, those two words changed my perspective. I saw immediately that the prospect of a new life, no matter the circumstances, was a reason to celebrate, not to cry.

That is the way it is with Elaine. She is my always, everywhere, good-time-or-bad-time adviser, supporter, friend.

I first met Elaine twenty-six years ago, when I was a brand-new wife and the nervous stepmother of four children, two of them rebellious teenagers. Elaine had already survived three teens, and she became my personal cheerleader, always giving me encouragement and good advice. When I struggled with feelings of inadequacy, she kidded me out of it.

"Teenagers are difficult creatures," she said. "Personally, I think they should be buried up to their necks in sand, fed and watered, and then dug up when they reach maturity."

In the first decade of our friendship, we argued. Our political views, then, as now, are completely opposite. I'm a Democrat. She's a die-hard Republican. We disagree on religious issues, and we have dissimilar styles when it comes to dealing with problems. But over time, our differences have blurred and faded. Now, as we struggle with disappointments and illnesses, we rely on each other. Caring about each other and laughing together is the lifeboat that keeps us afloat in a sea of daily troubles.

It is impossible not to laugh with Elaine. The woman is a magnet for the weird. Years ago, a kid followed her home from a restaurant because he liked her toenail polish. Her husband, while upset, wasn't surprised. Strange things happen to his wife.

One morning, she was driving her kids to school in her bathrobe, dropped a cigarette (she smoked then), and set herself on fire. She had to jump out of the car and fling off her nightclothes to save herself. She had a similar experience the night she called the paramedics because she thought her husband was having a heart attack. She dialed 911, rushed downstairs to open the door, and then raced back upstairs to see about her husband and change clothes. As soon as she got the nightgown over her head, she saw a dumbfounded paramedic standing in the doorway. She and her husband recovered, but she still groans when she remembers it.

Both of us, like most women our age, have lost our mothers. My mama died years ago, and Elaine's mom has slipped into the gray world of Alzheimer's. Without realizing it, Elaine and I have become mothers to each other. We do all the little things to comfort each other that our mothers would have done. As only women can, we understand the despair of aging; how trying on bathing suits under a fluorescent light can be devastating; and how age spots make you feel ugly. When I complain about the indignities I discover in the mirror, she always one-ups me.

"I have crow's feet the size of Big Bird's tracks," she kids. "Don't fuss about your wrinkles. The important thing is that we're still on this side of the dirt."

Through good experience, I've learned to trust her advice. In 1984, my husband and I were agonizing over buying a dream house we had stumbled onto. It was expensive, and I was really scared to commit to the debt.

"Life is short," she said. "You never know what's around the corner. Go for it."

We bought the house, a perfect hideaway on a beautiful lake, and it has been a constant source of joy to the entire family. Next to getting married, my husband and I agree that it is the best decision we ever made.

Now and then, my friend brings me back to reality when I get overanxious about trivial things. She reminds me that I'm just human and that it's okay to be frivolous.

Recently, I called her when I had an attack of temporary insanity.

"I've done the stupidest thing," I said. "I bought a giant compote of two monkeys holding up a shell. It's not even genuine majolica, and it cost a lot. What was I thinking?" I wailed.

"Quit beating yourself up," she said. "Seeing

those monkeys will make you smile every single day. Who can put a price on that?"

But Elaine has done more than encourage me. She has inspired me. With her bountiful spirit and unfailing dedication to accomplishing good, she has become my gold standard. Her responses to people in need, whether it's an old man working as a bag boy or a child who can't afford books, are instinctive and generous. She lives her biblical principles. When I'm challenged to go the extra mile, I think about my friend, and I do it.

Amazingly, Elaine needs me as much as I need her. This is a difficult time in her life. Her husband suffers from an incurable lung condition, and three of her grown children have life-threatening illnesses. At least twice a day, she goes to the nursing home to care for her mother, even though her own health is poor. Knowing the strain she is under, her brother, who lives in another state, asked how she is able to keep going.

"I have one true friend who loves me, warts and all, and who will never, ever let me down," she said.

It was the best compliment I have ever received.

—*Rochelle Lyon*

These Small Things

My mother reads the newspaper in bed at night. Propped up on pillows and reading glasses perched on the end of her nose, she makes a pleasant rustle with the turning of pages, the folding of sections, in the quiet of her bedroom at home. I think this has been her ritual forever, but I can't be sure.

Tonight, she is sleeping in my house, borrowing my son's bed, reading my newspaper, which is different from hers. She finds this interesting and tears out an article from the health and fitness section about the power of cranberries to fight bad bacteria in the digestive tract.

While she reads, I walk into and out of the room, making more trips than necessary to my son's dresser for fresh underwear and library books as I ready the children for bed. Truth be told, I just want to hear that rustle, to see her pink satiny slippers with the

little bows sitting on the floor by her suitcase, to
smell her creamy ready-for-bed scent, so oddly out of
context in a bedroom decor of home-run hitters and
dinosaurs.

She has come to give me a dose of comfort and
companionship in the middle of a five-day stretch in
which my husband is traveling on business, and I am
grateful for it down to my bones.

I'm grateful as I rise for the umpteenth time from
our supper, a supper she has prepared, to fetch some
critical item for my three-year-old daughter—catsup,
the polka-dotted fork, no, the other polka-dotted
fork, more apple juice.

I'm grateful as she loads the dishwasher while I
take a call from my husband in Chicago, who is kind
enough not to mention the piano bar he and his
hard-working colleagues are preparing to visit after
dinner at a good restaurant. (I learn of these things
only after he is home and only if I ask—wise man.)

I am grateful when she graciously agrees to four
quick games of Clue Junior with my seven-year-old
son after supper, and when she discreetly busies herself with some small thing in her room while I attempt
to handle my red-haired daughter's fatigue-induced
tantrum. (Whose fatigue induced the tantrum, I
wonder as I write this, my daughter's or mine?)

"These are precious years for you, but they can
wear you out in a hurry, can't they?" she sympathizes

when we finally have a moment to talk. I am lying next to her in bed for a little while, being a daughter instead of a mom.

"You managed with four," I say in wonderment, staring at the ceiling.

"Oh, but they were spread out more. I had help from the older kids."

This is only partially true. My siblings were seven, eight, and twelve years old when I was born. And when Dad was working all day and earning his degree at night on the G.I. bill, they were busy toddlers. (She once told me that for four years she ironed two white dress shirts each day for my dad: one for work and one for night school.)

She is just being kind.

I rearrange the Goosebumps pillow under my head and think about what I always think about when my husband travels and I am managing the household and the family alone: single parents and how they manage to do it every day, every night, every weekend.

"I'm glad you're here tonight," I say and squeeze her hand.

"I love to be here," she squeezes back.

In the morning I bring a steaming cup of coffee to her bedside. She relishes it like nectar from the gods.

"Do you know how long it's been since someone brought me a cup of coffee in bed?" She sighs, taking her first sip with obvious pleasure.

"I thought Dad always brought you coffee in bed," I say, surprised.

"No, he doesn't know how to operate the new coffeemaker."

I make a face. "This is the same man who in his early seventies learned how to operate his own computer, modem and all."

We shake our heads and giggle in the gray morning light. Then I'm off to answer my daughter's call from the steps, where she is stretching and singing "Old McDonald."

The next day my mom and I talk on the phone. She's back home, planting tulip bulbs and making chicken-vegetable soup. I give her a play-by-play of my day. She *mm-hmms* and *tsks* in all the right places.

"Thanks for coming up for the night, Mom," I say again before we hang up.

"Thanks for bringing me coffee in bed," she says, and means it.

—*Marsha McGregor*

Little Big Woman

I had just poured myself a cup of coffee and dropped into a chair at the kitchen table. My daughters, Carla and Elaina Marie, were off to school, and my husband, Carl, was off to work. Each morning, the woodsy scene on Caney Mountain came alive as the sun crept down the side, chasing the dark with a cheery shade of raspberry. I always took time to enjoy the drama before beginning the day's chores on our small farm.

Then I saw it. Thick, black smoke billowed into the sky from Caney Mountain. Sparks spit through the treetops in the early morning mist.

"Miss Natalie's house is on fire!"

In a panic I slammed down my cup, spilling coffee, and flew out the door. I raced down the hill past the wide-eyed cattle. Seeing me coming, they had lined up like soldiers to watch. I scrambled over the hog-wire fence and galloped across the road that snaked along the valley floor.

"No time to take the driveway!" I puffed, and plunged into the woods leading straight to Miss Natalie's house. My mind raced. "Poor Miss Natalie. She's probably still asleep. Overcome with smoke by now. The whole sky looks black from here!"

Mountain laurel brushed at my face; blackberry briars scratched my arms and snared my clothing. "Almost there!" I wheezed. The smoke pressed in, limiting my vision. Suddenly, an ear-splitting roar vibrated through the sooty shadows. I pulled up short and stared. Miss Natalie was sawing a downed jack pine into stove-wood lengths. A brush pile burned farther uphill. Open-mouthed, I watched, too relieved to be annoyed that my legs felt like oatmeal and my heart boomed in my ears.

At that moment, Miss Natalie discovered my haggard figure and jumped back, startled. "Goodness, Joyce, you scared me. You okay? You look awful. Why are you wearing your robe and pajamas?"

"I, uh . . . thought, uh . . ." I stopped and sucked in a breath. "I thought your house was on fire!"

"Goodness, no!" She giggled. "I'm just burning a little brush. How do you like my new chainsaw? I bought it so I could clear out some of these old jack pines. The woods are cluttered with them, don't you think?"

"Yeah, I guess so." My flushed face began to cool, and my pounding heart to slow. I flung out my arms and turned toward home, stumbling over fallen logs I must have jumped over on my way up. I forced my unwilling legs to carry me back across the road and up the hill. The chainsaw roared to life again.

"None of your business!" I hissed at Sweet Pea, our milk cow, who was still rooted to the ground, gawking. "Come to the barn, you old witch! I have to milk. Now!"

Warm milk streamed into the bucket. "A chainsaw! At her age! Sixty-eight if she's a day; maybe seventy!" I leaned my head into Sweet Pea's flank, trying to relax. I really shouldn't have been surprised. Carl, who's known Miss Natalie all his life, takes her wild and stormy nature in stride. To those who don't know her well, she's a frail little lady with angel wings who could persuade anyone to bungee-jump from a cloud. To me, she's a never-ending source of amazement.

Miss Natalie's neighbors love her, even after two of them wrestled her new 300-pound Buck stove into her tiny house. Even after others had installed her new sink and cabinets from Lowe's. Even after poor young Greg inched her new organ from the truck bed, across the porch, and through the door. "Fine boy," she commented. "Good neighbors in this community. I'm proud to live here."

Carl and I had decided to build our own house after discovering how much interest was tacked onto a loan.

"Good," said Miss Natalie. "I'll help."

Two days before construction was to begin, her red Jeep truck bounced up the driveway and slid to a halt, barely missing the split-rail fence and the kids' pet rooster, Roho.

"Where do I start?" she asked, tying on a Harris Hardware apron and taking up her favorite blue-handled hammer. Every day, Miss Natalie hammered, sawed, sanded, peeled logs, and planed lumber. When work slowed, she swept up sawdust and burned debris. When it came time to finish the kitchen, she said, "You go on now, Joyce, and do something else. I'll handle this." Two days later she had sized and nailed up more than a hundred pieces of four-inch poplar board paneling.

One morning, I was stacking lumber when Miss Natalie's bespectacled face appeared over the edge of the roof, forty feet up. "Bring me those roofing tacks, Joyce. I need to fill my apron."

"Not on your life," I gasped, getting dizzy just looking up.

Carl shouldered the box of nails and climbed the

ladder. Together they threw row after row of shingles into place. In two days, the job was done. Miss Natalie nailed the last one down.

"There!" she declared.

A fire blazed in the fireplace of our new house. Miss Natalie and I relaxed in comfortable silence, but I was aware of the wheels turning in her head.

"Do you think Carl could find a cow for me? A nice little Jersey? They give lots of cream. I could churn and make butter. I'll build a little barn and clear some brush for an electric fence."

I stared at her. "A cow?" When would I stop being surprised?

"Cow!" Carl yelled when he heard. "How can she milk a cow with her arthritic hands?"

"She'll manage," I stated. "She always does."

"Yeah, I guess," he said.

"She still has the pioneer spirit," I offered.

"Hmm! All she needs is a musket and a coonskin cap."

Blam! Blam! Gunshots echoed across the valley. "Uh, oh, what now?"

I finished hanging clothes on the line and hurried to answer the phone.

"Joyce, want to come for lunch?"

"Don't tell me. . . . It's squirrel season?"

"Right. Nice and fat."

"I'd love to," I said. "Did you wear your coon-skin cap?"

"Pardon?"

"Never mind. I'll be over at noon. Thanks."

The fried squirrel was delicious. Watching Miss Natalie scurry around the kitchen flinging things on the table, I realized why all young folks like her so much. While other people her age grow old, Miss Natalie remains young.

My husband, two children, and I hurried into our best clothing one Sunday morning and headed off to church. As we drove down our driveway, we saw Miss Natalie—stretching to see over the dashboard—drive by in a cloud of dust. Her new Buick with its plush sheepskin seat covers flashed by, hardly more than a red streak against the gray pavement.

"What a transformation!" I said. "On Sundays, she lays aside all work and dresses like the Queen of Sheba, all bejeweled and made up."

"I want to be just like her when I grow up," declared Carla from the backseat.

"Me too!" piped little Elaina Marie.

I understood why. She spills over with hope and wonder and finds secrets everywhere. Her yard preens itself in a profuse array of flowers. She is a woman of farm, earth, and work. Her brain brims with knowledge of herbs and healing and of wisdom born of communication with Creation. She tries her hand at watercolor art, too, and would fly with it if she had an ounce of patience.

The Bible speaks of the light of the Lord's smile on certain people. I think He laughs outright when He observes Miss Natalie. Goodness knows God Almighty is the only one she listens to. She is steered by a star, with a faith that rises higher than Caney's summit—right up to heaven.

As I write this story about my mother-in-law, Natalie Matilda Barnett ("Granny" to the kids), I wonder if the names and places should be changed. The neighbors are growing curious about the identity of the little old lady in shorts, Nike sneakers, and sunglasses speeding up and down the road on a flashy new ten-speed bike. It's red.

"We can't imagine who she is," we declare.

—*Joyce Lance Barnett*

Fly Away

The sky was clear beyond the vanishing snow, giving rise to the sweet scent of spring. Above, a flock of geese was making its way home. From the vantage point of her car seat, my four-year-old studied the geese with great curiosity.

"Is the mommy bird sad when her babies grow up and go away?" she asked with a child's wisdom that startles a parent.

The prescience of this little girl with puffy cheeks and huge brown eyes staring into my rearview mirror caught me by surprise. At age forty, I was at the cusp of midlife, and time had become a precious commodity. I had been mentally checking off our afternoon's list of errands, calculating the next few hours before that magical stroke of the clock pronounced the children's bedtime—and my freedom. Suddenly, with her simple question, I realized that time was running out for this unique partnership I had taken for granted. Soon, too soon, running to the dry cleaners, stopping by the office supply store, lunching at the mall, or browsing for books (where I bartered a new sticker book for extra time at the adult fiction table) would eventually become a solo turn.

I sighed at the barren landscape ahead. After all, she is my youngest child. She would be the last to accompany me to the grocery store, requesting a cookie from a friendly cashier or challenging my patience with those dreaded words, "I have to go potty." "Now?" I would cry out, glancing at our groceries on the conveyor belt, then at the person ahead waiting to have a check approved. Heads would turn in the direction of the middle-aged woman carrying her tot like a football while making the hundred-yard dash across the store to the ladies' room. "When will this day end?" I'd moan, exhausted, returning to find that the manager had restocked my abandoned food.

Driving to that same market on the day the geese caught her attention, I didn't want the day to end. I admit: It is a one-sided proposition. She goes where I go, does what I do, without much choice in the matter. But she is always game. Who else would stand in line at the post office with me for half an hour with only the promise of a lollipop as compensation? We are a twosome, she and I, recognized as such in the places we haunt. After all, what would

Laurel have been without Hardy? Batman without Robin? Winnie without Piglet? A lump rose in the back of my throat.

"Mommy," she said. "You didn't answer my question."

My gaze followed the birds disappearing over the horizon. Maybe their joy was in watching their young learn to fly, knowing they had shared those lessons together. For us, too, there would be new experiences to share as each season passed. She, too, would develop independence, travel secure in the space she has been given.

"The mother bird feels proud of her children," I answered. "How about we stop at Blockbuster?"

I looked over my shoulder to see her grinning in the backseat. And I sent up a silent prayer that in the years to come, when she has left the nest, I'd remember this moment. Someday, releasing her into the world might take her far from me. But for now, we're still the dynamic duo.

—Tracy Williams

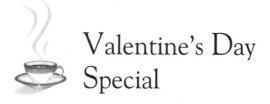

Valentine's Day Special

As I opened the shop door, a bell overhead chimed to announce my arrival. Once inside, I took a deep breath to savor the aroma of rose and lavender potpourri.

Then, accompanied by the strains of a classical harpsichord piece playing softly on the stereo, I made my way toward the rear, bypassing vintage clothing and racks of secondhand jeans, sweaters, and dresses. I paused to look into an oak and glass display case filled with antique necklaces and earrings.

Finally I reached the "sitting room," which displayed Victorian antiques: a burgundy velvet settee, wooden rockers, braided rugs, lace doilies, and some ferns thrown in for effect.

Along the far wall sat a crowded rack of wedding gowns.

There I was, a thirty-something woman who had

returned to college after my divorce, and I couldn't afford a new gown for my second marriage. I hesitated for many long moments, though. The thought that someone else had been married in these dresses was not at all appealing to me.

Finally, I decided it wouldn't hurt to at least *look* at the secondhand gowns.

But what was I doing here, anyway? On a weekday and Valentine's Day, besides. I drove past the shop every day on my way to and from the university, and I really don't know what compelled me to stop at Reflections of the Past that afternoon.

My fiancée Randy, and I were planning to be married in four months, after we both graduated from college. But instead of feeling happy, as I walked toward the gowns, I felt lonely. It was Valentine's Day, after all, and Randy was 150 miles away, attending classes at a different university. I had been sure I would never get married again after I divorced my first husband, but then I met Randy. And now we were engaged.

Of course we were looking forward to our wedding day with great joy. But we didn't have much money between us. College—living expenses, tuition, books, and materials—had seen to that. Even the small cars we drove, each with nearly 150,000 miles on it, attested to the fact that we were just barely getting by.

I always teased Randy by telling him that at least he knew I was not marrying him for his money. And I had already reconciled myself to buying a practical dress that I could wear for other occasions, just as I had done for my first wedding.

"It doesn't matter what you wear," Randy said whenever I bemoaned the fact that I would not have a "real" wedding dress. "You'll be the most beautiful bride in the world to me—even if you're wearing a burlap bag with holes cut for the neck and the arms."

As I began looking through the gowns, once again I reminded myself that a real wedding dress wasn't important. I didn't want to wear a second-hand gown anyway. And yet, I grew increasingly disappointed when I realized none of the dresses were my size. An 18 would do if I suddenly gained quite a few pounds. I hadn't worn a size 5 since I was in seventh grade . . . if then.

"May I help you?" asked a voice from behind me. It was the woman who owned the shop.

"Well," I replied. "I don't really see anything here. . . ."

"Oh," she said. "That's a shame."

She paused for a moment, deep in thought.

"Wait. I've got another one hanging in the back. Just came in today. I'm not even sure what shape it's in—"

She disappeared without waiting for my reply. In a few minutes she returned, struggling to keep a long, white gown off the floor. I could already see that the dress had too much lace and way too many ruffles to suit my taste.

The woman laid it across the burgundy velvet settee. "Why, this is in excellent shape," she noted, fingering the lace. "It's a size 12. Will that work?"

Although I really did not want to try on the gown, I found myself in the fitting room with it. The woman was only trying to be helpful, and I didn't want to hurt her feelings.

I slipped the dress over my head and struggled to close the long zipper in the back. When I turned to look at my reflection in the full-length mirror, my first reaction was confirmed. A huge satin ruffle and ridiculously puffy sleeves dominated my upper body while limp folds of lace clung to my legs.

"Here," said the woman, pushing a hoop slip under the fitting room door. "It needs a slip."

A hoop slip? Who wears hoops anymore?

Once again, I wrestled with the dress, tussling with the fabric until the slip was in place and I could arrange the full skirt over it.

I turned to look in the mirror.

Frothy rows of lace ruffles cascaded gently to the floor. And now that the skirt had achieved its proper proportions, it balanced the puffy sleeves and the satin ruffle around my shoulders, making me look like I had Scarlett O'Hara's waist.

I thought of rose gardens and parasols.

And then I pictured myself walking down the aisle of the little country church by the lake where our wedding would take place. The church was appropriately named Heart Prairie, and it had been built by Norwegian immigrants during the 1800s. Separated from my roots, living 250 miles from where I had grown up in west central Wisconsin, I felt a bond with the little stone church and the people who had built it so long ago. My grandparents and great-grandparents had been Norwegian immigrants. The wedding gown would look stunning against a background of gleaming hardwood and the black wrought-iron sconces that held oil lamps—the church was still lit the same way it had been when the Norwegian immigrants attended services there.

Still, the idea that some other woman had been married in this dress bothered me.

"Come out so we can see," said the owner of the shop.

Wondering who "we" referred to, I emerged from the fitting room. A small crowd stood off to one side. The shop owner. A clerk. Three customers. And a little girl with long dark curly hair.

"Ooooohh, it's perfect!"

"She'll be a beautiful bride in that dress."

"It's like it was made for her!"

"Mommy, can I wear a dress like that when I grow up?"

"Do you like it?" asked the shop owner. "The dress is about twenty years old, I think, although it's been kept perfectly."

"It's really a lovely gown," I said. "But I can't wear—I don't want to wear—a dress that's already been worn. And it's not that so much, either, but it was worn by somebody I don't even know. If it was my mother or my sister . . ."

As my voice trailed off, the clerk and the owner looked at each other. The owner reached into her pocket and held out a slip of paper she had found pinned in the bottom of the garment bag.

I glanced at the note. "Never been worn," it read.

"We're not sure of the exact circumstances," said the owner.

"The wedding was probably called off after the dress was ordered and fitted," added the clerk.

It took me about five seconds to make up my mind. I bought the gown. The price was probably one-fifth the cost of a new gown from a bridal shop.

"Happy Valentine's Day!" said the owner when I turned to leave.

"Thanks," I replied, smiling.

"And be sure to bring in some pictures of your

wedding," added the clerk. "We'd love to see them."

"I will," I promised.

As I walked out to my car, I could hardly wait to get home so I could call Randy. I knew just what I was going to say: "Sweetheart, you'll never guess what I found. I won't be wearing burlap after all."

—LeAnn R. Ralph

Sharp Eyes

When I was five years old, my mother awakened me one sticky summer night.

"I want to show you something," she whispered.

She pushed my damp hair out of my eyes and hauled my limp body up from a nest of sweat-soaked sheets. I rested my cheek on her shoulder, burying my face in her fuzzy blue bathrobe. She carried me through the house, out the back door, and onto the patio. She sat in a green lawn chair and cradled me in her lap, wrapping an afghan around both of us to discourage the mosquitoes.

"Look," she said, pointing at the sky.

I rubbed my eyes and looked. At first I saw only the constellations, whose names she had taught me: Orion the Hunter, the Big Dipper, the Seven Sisters. Then I saw what she was pointing at. Dozens of stars fell from the sky, trailed by sparks of light. I stared open-mouthed, wondering if all the stars might disappear forever.

"It's a meteor shower." My mother explained that meteors were pieces of rock much closer to the Earth than the stars.

"Will they hit us?" I asked, covering the top of my head with my arms.

She smiled. "No, but they're pretty to look at, aren't they?"

I nodded and continued to gaze up at the light show. My eyelids grew heavy, and I fell asleep in her arms. I woke only for a moment, when she lowered my head onto my pillow and kissed my forehead.

My mother always went out of her way to show me things. I was the only child in my kindergarten class who could tell a sparrow from a starling, a pansy from a petunia. Every car trip was an adventure with her. Weeds became wildflowers, clouds became thunderheads, and shadows moving through the trees became deer. When I was the first to spot a badger scurrying into the brush at the side of the road, she told me I had sharp eyes.

When I was thirteen, my sharp eyes turned inward. I sat in the backseat of the car, my ears covered with headphones. I pretended my mother was my chauffeur. I cared more about the pounding music and the pimples on my face than I did about stars and badgers.

She made sure that I came outside one night to see a lunar eclipse. She didn't have to wake me up that time.

I looked at the inky circle superimposed upon the moon and said flatly, "Very nice."

"Isn't it beautiful?" she said, handing me her binoculars. She didn't seem to notice my sarcasm.

She was showing things to other children by then. Her first-grade classroom overflowed with nests, bones, leaves, and shells. One winter night, I cooked dinner for my father while my mother stayed at school to host her annual Star Gazing Party. I pictured her standing outside on the frosty grass of the playground with her students and their parents, showing them Orion the Hunter, the Big Dipper, the Seven Sisters. Afterward, they would go into the classroom for hot cocoa and cookies.

Her face was flushed when she came home. I stood at the kitchen sink, elbow-deep in suds. She asked me if I'd seen the sky.

"No, I've been doing dishes. And now I have to do my homework."

She waved me away with a dishtowel, plunged her hands into the steaming water, and scrubbed at a skillet. "Take a look if you get a chance. It's so clear out tonight."

I stomped to my bedroom and, glaring, turned my sharp eyes to the textbooks strewn across my bed.

One spring evening when I was twenty-six, my mother called. "You have to see it. It's incredible! And there won't be another comet this close in our lifetime."

I told her I couldn't see any stars where I lived. The night sky glowed orange in Los Angeles.

She sighed. "Well, it's still clear and dark up here at night. Why don't you come and visit this weekend?"

I told her I couldn't get away, that I had too much work to do. My sharp eyes were occupied with copyediting magazine articles. I had to obliterate every misplaced comma and dangling participle I saw. I couldn't afford to spend my evenings searching the skies for comets. But when I hung up the phone, I felt bad about missing something she had taken the time to point out to me.

Two nights later, as my husband and I walked toward the car after a movie, I looked up into the cool, salty air, and I could actually see a few stars. One of them looked fuzzy. I took off my glasses, thinking they were smeared, but they were fine. I suddenly realized what I was seeing.

I grabbed my husband's arm. "Look, it's the comet!"

We watched it from the car windows all the way home. I rested my cheek against the cold glass and wondered if my mother was looking at it, too. I couldn't wait to call her when we got home.

Now my mother is old. She lives in a nursing home and cannot hear my voice unless I shout directly into her left ear. When I visit, I ask her if she'd like to go outside to see the stars. She nods. I help her into her wheelchair and pile several quilts on top of her so she won't get chilled. I push the wheelchair into the courtyard and show her the constellations, whose names I learned so long ago: Orion the Hunter, the Big Dipper, the Seven Sisters. Her gnarled index finger is shaky, but her sharp eyes know exactly where to look.

—*Madaleine Laird*

Fairy-tale Endings

All true fairy-tales begin "Once upon a time." And so must this love story, which began more than two decades ago.

An Oregon writer met a Stockholm doctor in a San Francisco restaurant, and they ended up touring the city together, walking and talking and talking and walking. The next weekend, he would be in Seattle, so she followed, walking and talking and talking. The two platonic friends parted, agreeing it was best not to write. As the woman drove south, she had the strange feeling of leaving her best friend.

Yet, they did write, and their letters crisscrossed in the mail and continued across the continents, sharing careers, families, philosophy, their mutual love of nature. Surely they would never meet again, so the letters were honest and without guile. Two years passed, and the Swedish doctor came to work in

Seattle for a year. The man and woman met again, and they began to fall in love. But he had a family to whom he was committed; she acknowledged that and honored his integrity. Once again, they reluctantly said farewell, and she went on to marry another.

Over the years, she would wonder about him, ponder the what-ifs and if-onlys.

Nearly two decades later, the woman had a dream. In the dream, the man stood in her kitchen with his wife. The wife, without sadness or anger, was turning her husband over to the woman. With a start, the woman awakened: What could this dream mean, and what on earth was happening in his life?

At the very same time on the other side of the world, the man typed the woman's name into the Internet. Nothing. For months, he browsed. And then on the other side of the globe, she typed in his. Finally, they connected. His wife had died. She had divorced. And neither had forgotten the other.

Once more, the letters, and now e-mails, crossed. Early one July morning, the woman got a call. She hadn't heard the man's voice in twenty years. He was at a medical conference in Denver! Within three hours, she was on a plane, risking everything on a spontaneous surprise visit. In a convention room filled with 300 people, she found him. Twenty years spun back in time, and they were young again; nothing had changed.

Nothing but circumstances, that is.

In early November, the man flew the woman to his Sweden home for a two-week visit that felt like a honeymoon.

They went shopping together to decorate the new home he had just built. They wound through the narrow, cobbled streets of Gamla Stan (Old Town Stockholm) and clambered four flights of a centuries-old building to meet his eighty-five-year-old mother, who greeted the woman with a hug. She met his three grown children, who thanked her for making their father so happy and presented her with a gift upon her departure. She met his best friends, and together they laughed like old companions.

Together, they visited the cemetery on All Souls' Night, when families light candles and small lanterns on the graves. He spoke of the numbness, the pain, the daily walk through the woods to this gray tomb-stone. At the wife's grave, the woman burst into tears: "I always wanted you, but not at this price, never at this price!" The man and woman held each other, and came to understand: "For all things, there is a season."

Each day, he brought her breakfast in bed. Once more, they walked and talked and talked, and the days were seamless, fluid, without effort. They cleaned and they cooked and they entertained. They listened to music and read aloud. They lit candles morning and evening against the cold November darkness. They traipsed the woods, and he showed her favorite places: the meadow that he and his wife, as young parents, had cleared late each spring for the children's Maypole festivities; the swimming rock; the enchanted hollow tree where the kids once played.

They threw supplies into a duffel bag and climbed into his boat for the hour-and-a-half trip through the Stockholm Archipelago of 24,000 islands to his century-old cabin. The Baltic suddenly turned angry and wild, and she clung tightly to keep from being thrown from the banging boat while he steered them safely on. I would trust my life to this man, she thought. I already am.

They hunkered in the one-room cabin while the wind pounded at the red plank door. As the corner fire warmed the room, they stripped off layers of clothing and loneliness. Candlelight reflected in the tiny windowpanes and in their eyes, alone together in that wilderness on the edge of the world.

Each day they laughed and loved and learned more about each other. Each day they marveled that life just couldn't get better. And each day proved them joyously wrong.

Then these two people who so savored living alone agreed they would live together. It was as obvious as eating and breathing. "We have two wonderful places to live, we love each other, and the rest is just details," the man said.

The woman nodded, confident that the Fates that had brought them together over twenty years and 6,000 miles wouldn't fail them now.

At last, after years of writing about other people's fairy-tale endings, the woman is living her own.

Wish me luck!

—*Jann Mitchell*

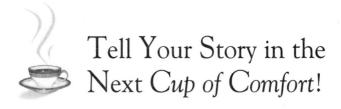

Tell Your Story in the Next *Cup of Comfort*!

We hope you have enjoyed *A Cup of Comfort for Women* and that you will share it with your mother, your daughter, your sister, and all of your female friends, coworkers, and neighbors.

We're brewing up lots of other *Cup of Comfort* books, each filled to the brim with true stories that will touch your heart and soothe your soul. The inspiring tales included in these collections are written by everyday men and women, and we would love to include one of your stories in an upcoming edition of *A Cup of Comfort*.

Do you have a powerful story about an experience that dramatically changed or enhanced your life? A compelling story that can stir our emotions, make us think, and bring us hope? An inspiring story that reveals lessons of humility within a vividly told tale? Tell us your story!

Each *Cup of Comfort* contributor will receive a monetary fee, author credit, and a complimentary copy of the book. Just e-mail your submission of 1,000 to 2,000 words (one story per e-mail; no attachments, please) to:

cupofcomfort@adamsmedia.com

Or, if e-mail is unavailable to you, send it to:

A Cup of Comfort
Adams Media
57 Littlefield Street
Avon, Massachusetts 02322

You can submit as many stories as you'd like, for whichever volumes you'd like. Make sure to include your name, address, and other contact information. We also welcome your suggestions or stories for new *Cup of Comfort* themes.

For more information, please visit our Web site: *www.cupofcomfort.com*

We look forward to sharing many more soothing *Cups of Comfort* with you!

Contributors

Ellen Jensen Abbott ("Monday Morning") lives in West Chester, Pennsylvania, with her husband, Ferg, and children, William and Janie. In the predawn hours when the house is quiet, she writes middle-grade and young-adult novels.

Beth Rothstein Ambler ("A Bike with Pink Ribbons") began her writing career when she ended her career as an executive and started a new life as someone with multiple sclerosis. She resides in New Jersey with her beloved husband, Chuck, whose rivals for her attentions are Butkus, her Labrador retriever, and Syco, her 160-pound rottweiler puppy.

Nancy Baker ("Enjoy!") retired in 1999 from Texas A&M University in College Station, Texas, where she was a program coordinator in leadership training. Since retirement, she has pursued her lifelong love of writing and has published several stories and articles. Married for forty-three years, she and her husband have three children, eight granddaughters, and three great-grandchildren.

Gail Balden ("The Christmas Box") is a writer on the Oregon coast, where she teaches Creative Journeys Writing Workshops for Women. Her work has been published in magazines, journals, and anthologies. She is currently working on a book about growing up in a small town in the Midwest.

Joyce Lance Barnett ("Little Big Woman") has lived her entire life on the farm where she was born in Mills River, North Carolina. There, she and her husband, Carl, raised their two daughters in a medley of horses, hard work, and mountain grandeur. An artist and writer, her work includes both word and pastel portraits of the people, the animals, and her three grandchildren who now enjoy these magnificent mountains.

Peggy Bird ("The Moon, Two Stars, and Italy") is a writer who lives in Vancouver, Washington. Her daughter, Meg, lives across the Columbia River in Portland, Oregon. They are planning to take Meg's daughter, Maggie, to Italy any day now.

Lauren Cassel Brownell ("Emily's Front Porch") lives in Newton, Pennsylvania, with her husband and two-year-old son. A freelance writer, she is currently working on a children's book and has published several magazine articles.

Renie Szilak Burghardt ("Two American Ladies") was born in Hungary and immigrated to the United States in 1951. She lives in the country, where she enjoys nature, reading, and family activities. Her writing has appeared in numerous publications, including *Whispers from Heaven, A Cup of Comfort,* and *A Cup of Comfort for Friends.*

Christine Caldwell ("A New Year's Magic") has recently completed her first novel, *The Complete Lily Lansing.* She is a graduate of Rutgers University, Camden, and lives in New Jersey with her husband, Mark McCarthy, and her daughters, Brooke and Jillian.

Talia Carner ("Riding the Rapids" and "Walking into the Wind") lives in Long Island, New York, with her husband and four children. Her personal essays have been published in *The New York Times,* anthologies, and magazines. Her novel, *Puppet Child,* will be released in summer 2002, and two others will follow in 2003. Before becoming a full-time writer, she was a marketing consultant to *Fortune* 500 companies and the publisher of *Savvy Woman* magazine.

Anne Carter ("Heart to Heart"), a native New Yorker, resides with her husband and precious feline on Long Island, near her children and grandchildren. Her inspirational stories have appeared in several major publications, and she is currently working on a collection of stories about her family's life experiences.

SuzAnne C. Cole ("The Table"), of Houston, Texas, is a former college English teacher who now concentrates on writing. She is the author of *To Our Heart's Content: Meditations for Women Turning 50* and other books, and her poetry, plays, and fiction have been published in magazines, newspapers, and anthologies.

Karen Deyle ("Traveling Companion") lives near the Finger Lakes region of New York surrounded by a loving family of choice. Her essays celebrate the joys of food, faith, friendship, and travel. A self-proclaimed travel fanatic, she keeps her backpack and passport by the door.

Hanna Bandes Geshelin ("A Hand to Hold") would be a full-time writer if she weren't sidetracked by homemaking, being Bubbe to her stepdaughter's daughter, gardening, volunteering in the local history museum, and visiting her elderly neighbors in Worcester, Massachusetts. Somehow, she still manages to write inspirational stories and to work on her fourth children's book.

Elizabeth P. Glixman ("Look in the Mirror, Darling") writes stories, essays, and poetry from her home in Massachusetts. She has a bachelor of fine arts degree in studio arts and a master's degree in education, and has worked in arts and education programs for children.

Sharon Hazard ("Joan's Lover") lives in Elberon, New Jersey. She wrote this story as a gift to her sister, Joan Tucker, who, in spite of her handicap, has always been an inspiration to Sharon.

Hedy Wiktorowicz Heppenstall ("Tree of Life") lives in Winnipeg, Manitoba. She is the writer-in-residence for the Manitoba Artists in Healthcare and cofacilitates a course called A Write to Joy. When her writing allows, she works as a nurse in a community health clinic.

Amanda Krug ("No Longer Strangers") lives in Fishers, Indiana, with her husband and four children. Her award-winning stories have appeared internationally in books, e-zines, and newspapers. She is currently coauthoring a book with Devasis Jena about an ancient tribal community in India.

Heidi Kurpiela ("Six Summers Ago"), of North Collins, New York, majors in journalism at Buffalo State College. She writes for two newspapers and works in a bookstore.

Madaleine Laird ("Sharp Eyes") is a freelance writer and editor whose credits range from how-to articles and book reviews, to personal essays and textbooks. She lives with her husband, Carl, in Canyon Country, California, where she uses her sharp eyes to spot roadrunners in riverbeds.

b.j. lawry ("Pink Organdy") was a reporter, feature writer, editor, and publisher of magazines and newspapers for thirty-six years. Retired now in the Arkansas hill country, she continues to write and has authored two published books, *Desert Heat*, a romance novel, and *The Piper of Featherly*, a mystery.

Rochelle Lyon ("A Little Taste of Heaven") is a homemaker and the matriarch to a large and ever-increasing family. She loves to write, and says that her home beside a small lake in Franklin, Texas, provides the perfect environment for reflection. She and her husband think it's the most beautiful place on Earth.

Donna Marganella ("The Women Who Made Me") has published short fiction and nonfiction, and favors humorous essays that reveal truths about contemporary life. By day, she is a high-tech marketing manager, but fails to see the humor in it. She lives in Carlsbad, California, with her husband, Kevin, who still laughs at her jokes.

Marsha McGregor ("These Small Things") is a freelance writer who lives with her husband, two children, and three cats in Hudson, Ohio. Her essays and articles have frequently appeared in *The Plain Dealer Sunday Magazine*. She also writes corporate and marketing communications for regional and national companies. Marsha is a member of the International Women's Writing Guild.

Robin Davina Lewis Meyerson ("The Wrong-Number People") is a former marketing communications director of a *Fortune* 300 company, who now works as an author, teacher, and speaker on self-improvement topics. She grew up overseas and currently lives with her family in Arizona.

Jann Mitchell ("Fairy-tale Endings") now lives a Cinderella life with her rediscovered Prince Charming near Stockholm, Sweden, and is learning Swedish. She and her prince travel widely and spend time in East Africa, where he works with AIDS patients and she sponsors a preschool. She is a freelance writer and motivational speaker.

Camille Moffat ("The Rising of the Sun") lives in the South and writes from her home on the side of a mountain overlooking the Shenandoah Valley. About her writing, she says, "I've always been grateful that I can write. After all, everyone needs a gift of some kind, and I'm a lousy cook."

Mary Jane Nordgren ("T Roses") is a retired teacher and family doctor now living with her husband (the principal in her book *Early: Logging Tales Too Human to Be Fiction*) in Forest Grove, Oregon. Their home overlooking snowcapped Cascade peaks often rings with the sound of children's laughter as they gather for family celebrations.

Barbara Nuzzo ("Camaraderie") lives with her husband, Ray, in North Brunswick, New Jersey. Her favorite pastime is traveling, which fits perfectly with her job as a travel agent. She'll go anywhere once, but is partial to France. An avid reader, she also enjoys writing and belongs to several writing groups.

Janet Oakley ("Technicolor Dreams") is the curator of education at Skagit County Historical Museum in LaConner, Washington, and teaches at a local college. She has published articles in historical journals and popular magazines, and has completed four novels. A recent widow with three grown sons, she still has dreams.

Marge Pellegrino ("Thanksgiving in Tucson") is a published author who leads creative writing workshops for all ages in libraries, schools, and other community settings. She resides in Tucson, Arizona.

Shannon Pelletier-Swanson ("The Truth about Dreams") is a freelance journalist, copywriter, and graphic designer. She also writes creative nonfiction and fiction. She shares a home with her husband, Ryan, and their identical twin daughters Presley and Shyann in Apopka, Florida.

LeAnn R. Ralph ("Valentine's Day Special") resides in the state of her birth and childhood, Wisconsin. A staff writer for two weekly newspapers, she also writes freelance stories about growing up on a dairy farm that her Norwegian great-grandparents homesteaded in the late 1800s. Her work appeared in *A Cup of Comfort for Friends* and *A Cup of Comfort*.

Barbara Rich ("The Mended Cup") relocated from the East Coast to Southern California more than twenty-five years ago. A semi-retired secretary, youthful grandmother, and newlywed, she loves interior design and storytelling.

Kimberly Ripley ("To Pearlie, with Love") is the author of *Breathe Deeply, This Too Shall Pass*, a collection of tales about the trials and triumphs of parenting teenagers, and a contributor to *A Cup of Comfort*. She lives with her husband and their five children in Portsmouth, New Hampshire.

Julie Clark Robinson ("A Solid Investment," "Boundless Gifts," "Demystifying the C-Word," "From Me to We," and "On Turning Forty") fuses what she sees with what she feels to write her oddly reassuring column, "Such Is Life." Her essays have been published in *Bride's Magazine* and *Family Circle*. Once an advertising writer and still David's wife and Reid and Jenna's goofball mommy, she can be found writing her heart out from their home in Hudson, Ohio.

Shaun Rodriguez ("Legend of the Perfect Girlfriend Girl") resides in Washington, D.C., with her husband and three children. A graduate of the Duke Ellington School for Performing Arts, she is an avid reader and lover of the arts. This is her first published work.

Therese Madden Rose, Ph.D., ("In My Mother's Heart") spent most of her life in Southern California. She is a special educator, psychotherapist, and writer. When she finds the time, she enjoys swimming, urban hikes, needlework, and traveling to visit her three adult children. She now resides on Long Island.

Julia Rosien ("Dishwashing Therapy" and "Well Furnished with Love") lives in Ontario, Canada, with her husband and four children. She teaches personal journaling and creative writing, and her essays have appeared in international magazines and newspapers. Words she tries to live by: "Happiness is a way, not a destination."

Nancy Scott ("Kneading the Bonds of Friendship") is an essayist and a poet with numerous bylines in regional and national publications, including *ByLine*, *Dialogue*, and *The Philadelphia Inquirer*. Two poems from her chapbook, *Hearing the Sunrise*, appeared in the disability anthology, *Staring Back*. She lives in Easton, Pennsylvania.

Lynn Seely ("My Time"), a nonfiction writer and book author, lives in Martinsburg, West Virginia, with her husband, John, and their two cats. The Seelys appeared on the television program *Miracle Pets* with Aggie, their heroic feline, the inspiration for Lynn's next book.

Pat Skene ("A Gift of New Beginnings") is enjoying her "arrivement" in the beautiful rural community of Cobourg, Ontario, Canada. She is an avid storyteller at the Ronald McDonald House and the Hospital for Sick Children in Toronto, Canada. Pat's first book, *The Whoosh of Gadoosh*, was released in June 2002.

Janie H. Starr ("Laura: Moving Friends Forever") holds master's degrees in public health and clinical psychology. In the mid-1980s, she left her private practice to work for issues relating to peace, justice, and community building. She has been a passionate speaker and writer on topics ranging from adolescent development and human sexuality to the nuclear threat, environmental sustainability, diversity, and now cancer, with her first published book, *Bone Marrow Boogie: The Dance of a Lifetime*, a memoir.

Sarah Stockton ("Steering into Safe Waters") lives with her family in the San Francisco Bay Area. A writer and the executive editor of Centered Path Publishing, she also teaches and mentors on spiritual writing and creativity.

Cheryl Terpening ("Chrysalis"), of Ann Arbor, Michigan, is an occupational therapist for the visually impaired. She has a twenty-two year-old daughter and a "brand-new" husband.

Gina Tiano ("The Trip to Plentiful"), originally from Santa Fe, New Mexico, is a freelance writer and humor columnist living in tropical McAllen, Texas, ten miles from the Mexican border. By day, Gina works with her husband at his mortgage company. By night, she dances the merengue and sips margaritas.

Peggy Vincent ("The Four Marys"), a retired midwife, is the author of *Baby Catcher: Chronicles of a Modern Midwife*, a memoir. She lives in Northern California with her husband of thirty-two years and her teenage son. Two adult children live nearby.

Sue Vitou ("Must Be Wednesday") is an award-winning writer with more than 200 published articles and essays. She lives in Medina, Ohio, with her four children, Matt, John, Brad, and Brenna.

Donna Volkenannt ("Julie's Gift") is a wife, mother, grandmother, godmother, sister, aunt, and friend. She lives in St. Peters, Missouri, and works for the Department of Defense. In her spare time, she enjoys reading and writing (but not arithmetic) and spoiling her grandchildren, Cari and Michael.

Davi Walders ("Duty-Free") is an award-winning poet, writer, and education consultant. Her poetry and prose have appeared in more than 150 publications, including *The American Scholar, Ms.*, and *JAMA*, and in numerous anthologies, including *Words: Contemporary American Women Writers* and *Beyond Lament: Poets of the World Bearing Witness to the Holocaust*. She developed and directs the Vital Signs Poetry Project at the National Institutes of Health and its Children's Inn for parents of children in treatment for life-threatening illnesses.

Dera R. Williams ("Quilting a Legacy") has resided in the San Francisco Bay Area for most of her life. She works in administration at a local community college. Her passion for researching her family's history has inspired her novel-in-progress.

Tracy Williams ("Fly Away") now works as a freelance writer after a career in newspapers, radio, and television. She lives in upstate New York with her husband, Robert, and daughters Lauren and Haley.

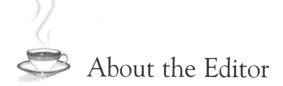 About the Editor

Colleen Sell has long believed in the power of story to connect us with our inner spirit, the Higher Spirit, and one another. She has always been particularly drawn to stories of passionate women who have followed their bliss.

The editor of more than fifty published books and the former editor-in-chief of *Biblio: Exploring the World of Books* magazine, she is also an essayist, journalist, screenwriter, and book author. When not spinning word magic, she enjoys a rural life in the Pacific Northwest, where she gardens, hikes in the woods, dances on the deck, and shares stories with family and friends.